BOOKS

Cloister Books are inspired by the monastic custom of reading as one walks slowly in the monastery cloister—a place of silence, centering, and calm. Within these pages you will find a similar space in which to pray and reflect on the presence of God.

COWLEY PUBLICATIONS is a ministry of the brothers of the Society of Saint John the Evangelist, a monastic order in the Episcopal Church. Our mission is to provide books and resources for those seeking spiritual and theological formation. COWLEY PUBLICATIONS is committed to developing a new generation of writers and teachers who will encourage people to think and pray in new ways about spirituality, reconciliation, and the future.

Loosening the Roots of Compassion

Loosening the Roots of Compassion

Meditations for Holy Week and Eastertide

Ellen Bradshaw Aitken

Cowley Publications
CAMBRIDGE, MASSACHUSETTS

Published in the United States of America by Cowley Publications, a division of the Society of Saint John the Evangelist. No portion of this book may be reproduced, stored in or introduced into a retrieval system, or transmitted, in any form or by any means—including photocopying—without the prior written permission of Cowley Publications, except in the case of brief quotations embedded in critical articles and reviews.

ISBN-10: 1-56101-244-0
ISBN-13: 978-1-56101-244-2

Library of Congress Cataloging-in-Publication Data

Aitken, Ellen Bradshaw, 1961–
    Loosening the roots of compassion : meditations for Holy Week and
Eastertide / Ellen Bradshaw Aitken.
        p.   cm.
    Includes bibliographical references.
    ISBN 1-56101-244-0 (pbk. : alk. paper)   1. Holy Week—
Prayer-books and devotions—English.   2. Eastertide—Prayer-books and
devotions—English.   3. Bible. N.T.—Meditations.   I. Title.
    BV90.A35   2006
    242'.35—dc22

                                                    2005028287

Unless otherwise noted, Scripture quotations are taken from the New Revised Standard Version of the Bible, © 1989, by the Division of Christian Education of the National Council of the Churches of Christ in the United States of America. Used by permission.

Quotations from the Psalms are from the
Psalter of the Book of Common Prayer 1979.

Scripture quotations signified AT are the author's translation.

Cover design: Rini Twait of Graphical Jazz, L.L.C.
Cover photo: Brand X Pictures, Getty Images
Interior design: Wendy Holdman

This book was printed in the United States of America on acid-free paper.

Cowley Publications
4 Brattle Street
Cambridge, Massachusetts 02138
800-225-1534 • www.cowley.org

For Bill

Contents

III. Incorporating the Resurrection

Preface

These meditations arise in part from a certain orientation to Scripture in its ancient environment and in our contemporary lives. Over the years the metaphor of the hologram has seemed to me an apt way of describing this orientation. A hologram preserves on a two-dimensional surface a three-dimensional image. As you tilt and turn the hologram, you come to see the image hidden seemingly below the surface. The approaches and questions of biblical scholarship provide us with a range of means to tilt and turn the scriptural text as though it were a hologram. They allow us to see in the text the indications, for instance, of its relationship to ancient communities of believers, certain convictions about the way the world works, or the traces of particular encounters with the divine. As together and alone we pray with scriptural texts, we tilt the hologram of the text with the questions and longings of our own lives.

We might also say that our lives are themselves holograms, which prayer, Scripture, the voices of our forebears in the faith, and others allow us to tilt. And the result of this tilting of the hologram is that we find within our lives dimensions of mystery, encounters with God, and the ground of desire that would otherwise be hidden from the surface.

It is of course also possible, and even welcome, to pray with Scripture amid an ever-expanding awareness of the text as belonging in the first place to an ancient people, a community of long ago. In doing so, we bring into our prayer ways of tilting the hologram, the text, that allow us to discern their perspectives on the world and their ways of engaging God. Such a practice then becomes an experience of encounter with the other, sometimes the familiar other, at other times the strange and difficult other. At its best, however, it is an experience that invites us into conversation with this other.

When we read Scripture in the liturgy and as we sing or say the psalms together, the contexts of our observance become a further and important way of "tilting the hologram." We hear a story, a piece of a theological discussion, a "word" of Jesus, a communal lament, a song of joy within the context of the eucharistic meal that we, as the baptized, celebrate together. The occasion of our gathering for the meal, for being in Jesus' presence, and for being nourished by Jesus' own self means that we bring certain questions to our hearing of Scripture. Nourished and shaped by our own eucharistic and baptismal experience, we ask in what ways the text bears witness to how another people in another time and place understood themselves to be sustained and renewed by their encounter with the divine. We tilt the hologram to discern patterns of sustenance, challenge, encouragement, and liberation—theirs and ours. We might glimpse, for example, in Jesus' words, "Consider the lilies of the field. . . . Do not worry, saying 'What will we eat?' or 'What will we drink?' or 'What will we wear?' . . . But strive first for the kingdom of God and its righteousness, and all these things will be given to you as well" (Matt. 6:28–33), a radically poor first-century community choosing dependence upon God's providence for their day-to-day needs. And we may then be challenged to seek out the ways we live by the gift of God: in the strength to go from day to day, the means to care for one another, or the insight to address the structural inequities of our society.

We tilt the text to find a fractal pattern of love, emerging sometimes with stunning clarity and at other times out of a set of convictions and perspectives that we do well to resist, mindful of the larger witness of God's mercy. We may notice that knit into the fabric of many biblical texts are the attempts of one group to define itself in opposition to another, often a group with whom it shares a great deal in common, thus dividing up the world between "us" and "them," or between "Jews" and "followers of Jesus." This drawing of boundaries is particularly fraught with the language of hatred in the stories of Jesus' death. Here we may tilt the hologram and see troubling perspectives and actions against a despised other, views that we would not want to adopt or condone. Yet at the same time, we perceive in the stories of Jesus' Passion attempts to root the Church in a love that knows no bounds.

The rhythms of the liturgical calendar provide even further ways of "tilting" the texts as we hear the texts in the context of seasonal practices and remembrances. The meditations in this book arose for me, as they may now for you, in the context of the observances of Holy Week and the first week of Easter. Many of them emerged from liturgical preaching in congregations for whom the communal remembering of Jesus' suffering, death, and resurrection during the Triduum was a central point

of reference as we reflected upon the suffering, injustice, and death we encountered on the streets of
our cities and in our own lives. The privilege of tilting the hologram of Scripture in these contexts has
been a great gift to me.

During the roughly ten years when these meditations took shape, I was also, in my academic
work, deeply engaged in research and teaching on
the traditions of Jesus' suffering and death in early
Christianity. This work shed particular light on how
some of the earliest ways of remembering Jesus'
death were shaped in and through the practices of
communities gathered for worship. The practices of
singing psalms and other familiar song texts from
the Scriptures of Israel combined with the retelling of the central stories of the Exodus and journey
through the wilderness into the Promised Land to
provide the language and frameworks for speaking of
Jesus' Passion. Jesus' death became for first-century
Christian communities the lens through which these
traditions were refracted. The rich range of these
ritual practices—what we have come to call baptism
and Eucharist—provided a set of prisms for refract-
ing these scriptural traditions retold now as ways
of remembering Jesus and as ways of constituting a
community around the memory of Jesus. My study,

meditation, and preaching on these same texts over the course of several Holy Weeks and Easters have thus emerged from the sense of a congregation's practices of remembering, a remembering both ancient and modern—integral to the incorporation of Scripture into our lives. The Maundy Thursday meditation, "A Rock of Refuge," thus grew out of the liturgy of foot washing and intense eucharistic devotion within a congregation weary from long caring for the poor and dying, yet also abiding in deep joy as they turned over their lives each week to God. For each of us, these experiences refracted the psalms of refuge and protection and the scriptural stories of miraculous food in the wilderness so as to highlight the constancy of divine love in the midst of suffering as a dimension of our common life.

I am thus appreciative of the generosity afforded me by the various Massachusetts parishes and congregations in which I was invited during a succession of Holy Weeks and Eastertides to share the ideas that form the basis of this book. In particular, I thank Saint Peter's Episcopal Church in Springfield, Saint Paul's Episcopal Church in Holyoke, the Paulist Center in Boston, the Society of Saint John the Evangelist in Cambridge, the Church of Saint John the Evangelist in Boston, and Harvard University's

Memorial Church. Conversations with friends, often preachers or scholars themselves, have enriched and refined my ways of tilting both ancient texts and the "texts" of our lives.

Composing such meditations is not unlike cooking a meal, and I am often grateful that those who receive them do not know all the details of what has gone on in the kitchen—the uncertainty about ingredients, the pots that boil over, the messiness of the creative process, the tasting of dishes partially prepared. In the preparation of this book, my husband, William Porter, has so often been willing to come into this kitchen early on and respond when I ask, "So what do you think is going on in this text?" or to taste, often late at night, a meditation that is almost prepared and to suggest perhaps a little seasoning here, a thickening of the sauce there. For his generous love and candid encouragement, I am grateful beyond words.

I offer these meditations now to you—out of my study (or kitchen) into the garden of your heart and prayer. They belong now to you, with my prayer and hope that they will help you to send forth deep roots from your life into Scripture and into the contemplation of Jesus' risen life. I would suggest that you read the meditations in tandem with the scriptural passages that inform them; in most cases the passages are provided at the outset of each reflection. Take what you need to help you pray your life and to discern new pathways of the resurrection in yourself and in the world around you—to loosen the roots of compassion within your heart.

I
Remembering the Resurrection
From Palm Sunday to Easter Day

Jesus Our Light

Palm Sunday

*This meditation is based on the reading of the Passion
Gospel from the Gospel of Matthew (26:36–27:66),
from which the following passage is drawn:*

Now at the festival the governor was accustomed to release a prisoner for the crowd,
anyone whom they wanted. At that time they
had a notorious prisoner, called Jesus Barabbas.
So after they had gathered, Pilate said to
them, "Whom do you want me to release for
you, Jesus Barabbas or Jesus who is called the
Messiah?" For he realized that it was out of
jealousy that they had handed him over. While
he was sitting on the judgment seat, his wife
sent word to him, "Have nothing to do with
that innocent man, for today I have suffered a
great deal because of a dream about him." Now

the chief priests and the elders persuaded the crowds to ask for Barabbas and to have Jesus killed. The governor again said to them, "Which of the two do you want me to release for you?" And they said, "Barabbas." Pilate said to them, "Then what should I do with Jesus who is called the Messiah?" All of them said, "Let him be crucified!" Then he asked, "Why, what evil has he done?" But they shouted all the more, "Let him be crucified!"

So when Pilate saw that he could do nothing, but rather that a riot was beginning, he took some water and washed his hands before the crowd, saying, "I am innocent of this man's blood; see to it yourselves." Then the people as a whole answered, "His blood be on us and on our children!" So he released Barabbas for them; and after flogging Jesus, he handed him over to be crucified.

Then the soldiers of the governor took Jesus into the governor's headquarters, and they gathered the whole cohort around him. They stripped him and put a scarlet robe on him, and after twisting some thorns into a crown, they put it on his head. They put a reed in his right hand and knelt before him and mocked him, saying, "Hail,

King of the Jews!" They spat on him, and took the reed and struck him on the head. After mocking him, they stripped him of the robe and put his own clothes on him. Then they led him away to crucify him.

As they went out, they came upon a man from Cyrene named Simon; they compelled this man to carry his cross. And when they came to a place called Golgotha (which means Place of a Skull), they offered him wine to drink, mixed with gall; but when he tasted it, he would not drink it. And when they had crucified him, they divided his clothes among themselves by casting lots; then they sat down there and kept watch over him. Over his head they put the charge against him, which read, "This is Jesus, the King of the Jews."

Matthew 27:15–37

A pillar of cloud by day—a pillar of fire by night. So God went before the people of Israel, leading them in safety out of slavery in Egypt, on dry land through the threatening waters of the Red Sea, and through the wilderness into the Promised Land (Ps. 78:13–16). A pillar of cloud by day—a pillar of fire by night; we know the story well! In one short week, we shall hear it told again, when we light the new light of Christ, the pillar of fire by which we remember how God has led us into the promised resurrection life.

But today from Matthew's Gospel, we read another story: the story of Jesus' suffering and death. Indeed, all this week we stand in the presence of this, the "great story" of the Church. Before the pillar of fire comes into our midst again, acclaimed three times as the "Light of Christ," the deacon will bring the hard wood of the cross before our eyes, proclaiming three times, "Behold the wood of the cross." And in these days, we will pray over and over again that we may walk in the way of the cross, in the way of Jesus' sufferings.

To hold the story of Jesus' sufferings and death in our midst is not an easy thing. We must consider carefully what it is we are asking when we pray that we may walk in the way of Jesus' sufferings. Like all the stories we tell, what we hear today has been shaped through the lives of the people who have held this story before us. It reflects their hungers, their struggles, their sorrows, and their convictions. For the evangelist Matthew, whose telling of the story we read today, the memory of the death of

Jesus is marked throughout by the experience of his church.

Of all the Gospels, Matthew's perhaps reflects the closest relationship between a Christian community and the Jewish community out of which it emerged, and from which it was now, at the end of the first century, quite recently separated. And all the marks of tension are there. For Matthew's church, the story of Jesus' death becomes a way of talking about their identity, just as it had for others before Matthew wrote his version, and just as it does for us. Throughout this particular telling of Jesus' death, we see the signs of an intimacy that is now estrangement. Responsibility for Jesus' death is laid at the hands of the Jewish leaders and of the crowd—no other Gospel casts the story in quite this way. And Matthew alone of the Gospel writers spins out a complex account of Judas's betrayal of Jesus. Here in Judas's betrayal, Matthew writes the experience of his community. Here, to borrow the words of the psalm, is the familiar friend, the man after Jesus' own heart, his companion, who broke bread with him and walked with him in the house of God—this most intimate of friends is now the adversary (Ps. 55:13–15). And so the relationship of Jesus and Judas mirrors the situation between

Matthew's church and the Jewish community of which they were once an intimate part. Yet note that we hear the story with its stark lines of innocence and blame from only one side of the estrangement. We hold this difficult history in our midst as one of the rememberings of Jesus' death that we have as our inheritance.

When we pray to walk in the way of Jesus' sufferings, it is not necessary for us to replicate the patterns of estrangement and pain that we inherit from our forebears in the faith. Although we acknowledge the reality of the ways in which they constructed the story, their ways of dividing up their world between the good and the bad, the friends and the enemies, do not have to be our ways. Indeed, we do not even have to divide up the world. We do not have to cast some groups—be they Jews or Muslims or other Christians or powerful governments or those who have harmed us or whom we have harmed—as the enemies of Jesus in order to receive the love God wants to give us. Indeed, in the strength of the love that God pours out abundantly upon the world and upon us, we are able to say "Never again" to some of the ways in which our ancestors have attempted to remember the death of Jesus, to ways that have involved the killing and contempt for those they have constructed as the enemies of Jesus. With God's help we can learn to say "Never again" to the ways in which Jesus' death and sharing in his sufferings have been used to justify the inflicting of pain upon one of God's creatures. But we continue to hold the memory of the death of Jesus in our midst; we continue to up-hold its centrality to our existence and identity; and we continue to pray that we may walk in the way of Jesus' sufferings. What does this mean? How are we to walk in Jesus' way without adding to the sufferings of the world which God loves so dearly?

Recall what Saint Paul and others affirm so strongly: that Jesus' death was indeed "once for all" (Rom. 6:10; Heb. 7:27). That is, Jesus' death is not repeated. We do not re-crucify Jesus during Holy Week in our liturgy or in our hearts. We do not need to fear that others will crucify Jesus. We do not need to use the Passion as an occasion to berate ourselves for all our sins, saying, "Jesus, it was I who crucified you." We do not need to hurt ourselves or others. No, the suffering of Jesus at that one time was enough, and we remember it and walk in the way of that suffering by some other route.

Let me put this a little differently. As you contemplate the story of Jesus' suffering and death, you might find that you are horrified at the human potential for violence and hatred exhibited in the act of putting Jesus to death. You might find yourself newly aware of the extent of such violence around us today: in the abuse of children or in the willful denial of how political decisions feed famine and epidemic. You, if you are like me, might find this awareness tugging at your own heart, asking hard questions about your own culpability either indirectly by your participation in society or directly by your own actions or failure to act. And you might in your prayer bring this awareness to the foot of the cross and find there the assurance that nothing is too horrible to stand in the way of God's presence. To do so is a fruitful way to let the contemplation of Jesus' Passion transform your life, more fruitful than berating yourself for Jesus' crucifixion. For when you condemn and thus hurt yourself, you so easily remain mired in your sinfulness, because it becomes a cherished way for you to enter into the story. Yet you are not the enemy of Jesus, but rather one to whom Jesus holds out the promise of life and lasting friendship.

The resurrection is the key. Through the ages

Christians have remembered Jesus' death as bringing about a new creation, a new way of being. Our ancestors in the faith talked about Jesus' death in terms of deliverance from oppression, of Jesus leading us into the land of milk and honey, of setting us in an open space, a space of salvation. And throughout the generations, Christian communities have attempted in faith—though sometimes getting it wrong—to learn to live this resurrection life.

To walk in the way of Jesus' sufferings, to walk in the way of the cross, is then to walk in the pathway of resurrection life that the cross opens to us. As the pillar of fire led the people of Israel safely into the Promised Land, so for us the cross opens up a way through the waters, through the wilderness. For us the cross and the pillar of fire, the light of Christ, become one. Jesus is thus the one who lights our way and defends us through the difficult and problematic parts of our lives, in the places where we may feel ourselves going astray. Jesus is also the one who knows our sufferings and shame most intimately—the cross tells us this—and so the pathway behind the cross is where we can bring our pain and there find an outpouring of love and healing beyond our imagining. And together as a community following in this way of suffering, we learn to shape our identity as a place of dignity for all, a place of justice, and to cultivate our common life as the place where God feeds our bodies and our hearts with the bread of angels.

Lead us, O good Jesus, by the light of your resurrection into ever-deeper remembrance of your cross and Passion, those mighty works of love whereby you are recreating our lives and indeed the whole world. When we walk in the wilderness of suffering and oppression, reveal your love—a love stronger than death—as our constant guide and companion. When we rejoice in the freedom that you give us, strengthen us with compassion for our sisters and brothers, the friend and the stranger, knowing that we are all nourished by the gift of your very self. Amen.

A Rock of Refuge

Maundy Thursday

For I received from the Lord what I also handed on to you, that the Lord Jesus on the night when he was betrayed took a loaf of bread, and when he had given thanks, he broke it and said, "This is my body that is for you. Do this in remembrance of me." In the same way he took the cup also, after supper, saying, "This cup is the new covenant in my blood. Do this, as often as you drink it, in remembrance of me." For as often as you eat this bread and drink the cup, you proclaim the Lord's death until he comes.

1 Corinthians 11:23–26

Now before the festival of the Passover, Jesus knew that his hour had come to depart from this world and go to the Father. Having loved his own who were in the world, he loved them to the end. The devil had already put it into the heart of Judas son of Simon Iscariot to betray him. And during supper Jesus, knowing that the Father had given all things into his hands, and that he had come from God and was going to God, got up from the table, took off his outer robe, and tied a towel around himself. Then he poured water into a basin and began to wash the disciples' feet and to wipe them with the towel that was tied around him. He came to Simon Peter, who said to him, "Lord, are you going to wash my feet?" Jesus answered, "You do not know now what I am doing, but later you will understand." Peter said to him, "You will never wash my feet." Jesus answered, "Unless I wash you, you have no share with me." Simon Peter said to him, "Lord, not my feet only but also my hands and my head!" Jesus said to him, "One who has bathed does not need to wash, except for the feet, but is entirely clean. And you are clean, though not all of you." For he knew who was to betray him; for this reason he said, "Not all of you are clean."

After he had washed their feet, had put on his robe, and had returned to the table, he said to

them, "Do you know what I have done to you?
You call me Teacher and Lord—and you are
right, for that is what I am. So if I, your Lord and
Teacher, have washed your feet, you also ought
to wash one another's feet. For I have set you an
example, that you also should do as I have done
to you.

John 13:1–15

On the coast of Maine, there is a particular cleft
in the rock, the place where long ago dark ba-
salt intruded into the hard granite and the granite
split. This ancient volcanic action has produced an
armchair in the rock, where one can sit surrounded
on three sides by low walls of stone and watch the
tide lapping the edge of the coast. I have sat often in
this armchair, from the day when as a young child
I first came upon it, and it is to this cleft in the rock
that I return in my mind's eye for strengthening, cer-
tainty, and refreshment. This is the place where, in
the words of Saint Patrick's Breastplate, "I bind unto
myself the stable earth, the deep salt sea, around the
old eternal rocks."[1]

I return to that place today as we read about

Jesus washing his friends' feet, and as perhaps we actually wash the feet of our neighbors. Sitting on that rock at high tide, you can dangle your feet, just up to the ankles, in the cold, brisk water of the Gulf of Maine. There you can let the waves break over your feet, washing away the sticky, hot sweat, refreshing the weary muscles, and cleaning your mosquito bites with astringent salt water. There the deep salt sea becomes a servant of God, offering our feet, weary from the journey and from work, cleansing and rest.

In the sanctuary that the cleft in the rock provides, and refreshed by the waves of the sea, I am able to remember. I remember the people and events of my life, I grieve, my heart warms, and, most of all, I am recalled to the steadfast, sure love of God. Embraced by that rock, I remember the times of protection and strengthening, even as the great salt sea reminds me of the call to venture forth, to take my part in that great company which labors in the loving purposes of God.

If you go to church tonight, most likely your liturgy will be one that speaks through and through of the refreshment and strengthening that God offers to us. This liturgy becomes the cleft in the rock—

that place of sanctuary—where we can remember in words and actions the love whereby God gives God's self to us in Jesus. It becomes the place where, remembering, we can seize that constant love and bind it to ourselves. In a certain sense, this liturgy shows us how we are to regard the events of the Passion and resurrection of Jesus, namely, that we are to remember this central story as a story of love offered freely to us, of a healing love that willingly joins itself to every place of suffering, horror, desolation, and pain within us and in this creation. And remembering this story, we are to seize this love, bask in its refreshment, and bind it upon our wounds.

Consider first the story of the Passover meal, told in Exodus 12. It is a meal for the journey, eaten hurriedly with sandals on your feet and a staff in your hand. It is a pilgrim feast—a meal given by God to strengthen the Israelites for the long, hard way out of Egypt, through the waters of the Red Sea into the wilderness. And consider the psalm, Psalm 78, recounting God's care for the Israelites in the wilderness: how God led them with a cloud by day and a pillar of fire by night. God splits the rock so that they may have water; God rains down manna upon them and gives them grain from heaven. Divine food—the bread of angels—given plentifully, abundantly to fill the deep need of the people. "Taste and see that the LORD is good" (Ps. 34:8).

Now *the rock* is perhaps not an immediately attractive metaphor for God, at least not to many modern ears. A rock is after all impersonal, fairly impassive, not particularly in touch with feelings and the like. But throughout Hebrew Scripture, the Rock is among the most important names or metaphors for God. The God of the covenant is the Rock who gave birth to us; the Rock is the name for God who rescues and protects the chosen, beloved ones. The Rock is a refuge for the oppressed and persecuted. Moreover, the Rock is the source of abundant refreshment: the source of water for the dry land and for thirsty bodies, of sweet honey, and of oil. The Rock followed the Israelites in the wilderness, just as the cloud and fire went before them. And Paul, as he began to write to the Corinthians about the Lord's Supper, reminded them that this Rock was Christ (1 Cor. 10:4).

For Paul, the Lord's Supper is the meal to remember and celebrate the new covenant: a covenant with the Rock who is Christ, the protector of the innocent, the refuge for the oppressed, and the source of manna and water in the wilderness. Into this covenant—indeed into this Rock, Paul would say—you have been baptized; this protection, refreshment, and healing strength are available to you. In the meal, the body of Christ is given for you. The cup of wine makes present to you the benefits given in the covenant—God's love that goes to every length to seek you out, God's work to forgive and re-create all that is past, and God's own presence to comfort and refresh you. And so it is for Paul that the community gathered for the Eucharist is constituted as the community in covenant with the Rock; the community becomes the Rock for one another and for the world—a community baptized into the covenant of love offered and love received.

Now, the evangelist John doesn't tell us much about refreshment from food—at least not in this Gospel text. (Elsewhere there is plenty about Jesus as the true bread from heaven and as the water of life nourishing and sustaining us.) But here we have Jesus washing the disciples' feet—a living example of the new commandment, "Just as I have loved you, so you also should love one another" (John 13:34). For John, this is the central commandment of the new covenant in Jesus—the consequence of remembering how God's love was manifested to the world in Jesus. The community is that place where renewing, refreshing love is offered and seized. Here God comes as the one who serves, who indeed actually desires to serve us, to wash our feet, to feed us.

Peter, of course, gives voice to the resistance that lurks in our own hearts: "You will never wash my feet" (John 13:8). Or as the poet George Herbert writes in "Love III": "Love bade me welcome: yet my soul drew back, / Guiltie of dust and sinne." But claiming the love that nourishes and refreshes us, the love for which we so desperately long, is our baptismal birthright: it is our inheritance as those who have been incorporated into the covenant with the Rock who feeds, refreshes, and protects us. What is more, this same God is already working in our hearts and bodies to enable us to accept that love ever more fully.

And so, through the words of Scripture and the liturgies where they are read today, we are invited in the actions that correspond to words to come to that living Rock, to that God who bears our pain and grief, and to turn over our dirty, tired feet and our hungry bodies to God's washing and feeding. We are invited in those actions to offer our souls that ache with griefs and fears and our hearts that bear the pain of others, to offer them to God for refreshment and healing. Come to this living Rock, and here taste and see that the Lord is good.

> *O God, the rock of our refuge, the wellspring*
> *of our refreshment, you bid us come to you*
> *when we are weary and heavy-laden, you*
> *welcome us when we are thirsty and hungry,*
> *yet you come to us before we can come to you.*
> *May your grace so work within us that we may*
> *not hesitate to come to you, to tell you our*
> *needs and our desires, and to claim the love*
> *that you show us most abundantly in Jesus.*
> *Amen.*

Abiding in the Cross

Good Friday

This meditation is based on the reading of the Passion Gospel from the Gospel of John (18:1–19:37), from which the following passage is drawn:

Then [Pilate] handed [Jesus] over to them to be crucified.

So they took Jesus; and carrying the cross by himself, he went out to what is called The Place of the Skull, which in Hebrew is called Golgotha. There they crucified him, and with him two others, one on either side, with Jesus between them. Pilate also had an inscription written and put on the cross. It read, "Jesus of Nazareth, the King of the Jews." Many of the Jews read this inscription, because the place where Jesus was crucified was near the city; and it was written in Hebrew, in Latin, and in Greek. Then the chief priests of the Jews said to Pilate, "Do not write, 'The King of the Jews,' but, 'This man said, I am King of the Jews.'" Pilate answered, "What I have written I have written." When the soldiers had crucified Jesus, they took his clothes and divided them into four parts, one for each soldier. They also took his tunic; now the tunic was seamless, woven in one piece from the top. So they said to one another, "Let us not tear it, but cast lots for it to see who will get it." This was to fulfill what the scripture says,

> "They divided my clothes among
>   themselves,
> and for my clothing they cast lots."

And that is what the soldiers did.

Meanwhile, standing near the cross of Jesus were his mother, and his mother's sister, Mary the wife of Clopas, and Mary Magdalene. When Jesus saw his mother and the disciple whom he loved standing beside her, he said to his mother, "Woman, here is your son." Then he said to the disciple, "Here is your mother." And from that hour the disciple took her into his own home.

After this, when Jesus knew that all was now finished, he said (in order to fulfill the scripture),

"I am thirsty." A jar full of sour wine was standing there. So they put a sponge full of the wine on a branch of hyssop and held it to his mouth. When Jesus had received the wine, he said, "It is finished." Then he bowed his head and gave up his spirit.

John 19:16–30

In the ancient hymn of the Passion, we sing, "Faithful cross! above all other, one and only noble tree."[2] Perhaps somewhere in your life there has been a special tree: a tree under whose shade you love to sit, a tree upon which you love to gaze from your window and watch the birds come to settle in its branches. Maybe it's a tree of your childhood from whose strong branch hung a swing. Or, it may have been a tree into which you climbed and sat, a tree with a tree house. In my imagination, I return to the low spreading euonymus tree in the front yard of the house of my early childhood. I have never had much of a head for heights and was daunted by the thought of climbing into the taller apple or maple trees. But this low tree with its wiry branches was just right. I could climb a few feet from the ground, nestle into the crook of the branches, and allow the tree's dense leaves to shelter me. Here the complexities of the adult world faded away; here I could dream and spin stories; here, as I stretched along a branch or swung down, I could feel the tree's strength flowing into me.

In God's great love for us, God gives us a tree. God gives us a tree that grows strong and vibrant at the very center of our life together. God gives us the cross, which the hymn extols for its faithfulness, its sweetness, and its tenderness toward Jesus. And this day, the hard wood of the cross is brought into our midst: we gaze upon it, revering the memory of God's faithfulness even in the place of brutal, shameful death, revering the way in which that faithfulness flows forth to us, to all the world, recalling through the wood of the cross the love that is stronger than death.

We come to the cross this day as the people of the resurrection, as a people joined to Jesus' risen life through our baptism. This reality about our lives, our identity, our community shapes how we approach the cross and how we remember that great central story of Jesus' suffering and death. And in remembering Jesus' Passion from the perspective of his resurrection and our own resurrection lives, we are doing what those first Christian communities and evangelists did as they crafted this mighty story of God's faithful perseverance. As they spoke of Jesus' death, they did so in the words of the psalms and the prophecies that told of God's solidarity with the suffering, God's steadfastness to covenantal love, and God's protection and defense of God's beloved people. As the earliest Christians reflected on how their own communities were gathered and shaped by Jesus' death and resurrection, they did so in terms of how God had carefully led the people of Israel through the wilderness, feeding them, giving them fresh spring water, and leading them always into the land of promise and freedom.

And so we too approach the cross, knowing our lives gathered into this marvelous constancy of God, knowing our bodies, our selves made one with Jesus' death and resurrection in our baptism. We approach the cross as the fount from which love pours out to us and upon us, recognizing it as a sign that God honors us and tenderly cares for us.

In her account of her visit to Jerusalem, the fourth-century pilgrim Egeria reports that beside the relics of the true cross stood two deacons, and the job of the deacons was to prevent reverent pilgrims from taking a bite out of the cross.[3] However humorous this seems to us, it nevertheless points to a kind of piety whereby people wanted to ingest, to take into themselves, this token of God's faithful love in the midst of suffering. Perhaps, as Julian of Norwich much later prays, by so doing they hoped to have a share in Jesus' sufferings—that is, to have a share in the way in which suffering and agony are transfigured by the presence of God.[4] They longed, just as you have perhaps longed, to take this love into themselves.

So God gives us this tree, this cross, so that we may find in it a fount of life and the love for which we long. God gives us the memory of Jesus' death and rising so that we may find our selves in that story. And because it is a difficult story, encompassing Jesus' rejection and abandonment, a trial and death caught up in political machinations, a painful death shameful in the eyes of the world, it is consequently a story that assures us there is nothing foreign to God, nothing that is outside the purview of God's love. It assures us that there is nothing in all human experience that cannot be gathered up in the love that prevails.

As we stand in the presence of this mighty story, as we approach the wood of the cross, as we come to Jesus, we bring our lives, and we offer Jesus all that we bear. We offer Jesus our hearts and bodies, and the stories of suffering and love inscribed upon them. We offer Jesus the problematic places of our lives and the prayers of our soul. We offer Jesus our fears—our fears of entering into his life, of engaging the pain and poverty of the world, of dying and abandonment, of loss and being shamed. We offer all this and more to Jesus, before the wood of the cross, knowing, even if only in the tiniest glimmer, that it is Jesus' desire to hold us, defend us, and tenderly enliven us. So we may also bring to the cross our hopes and our thanksgiving, honoring God for love so faithfully shown. And as we come to this tree of life, we may perhaps permit Jesus to honor us for the ways in which we have engaged his life, for how we have allowed our lives to be places where the mercy of God shows forth.

In my imagination, our stories, our selves, and all that we bear are nestled into the branches of the cross, like a small child perched in the strong branches of a tree. I pray God to hide us in the wood of the cross, to let us find a home, a nesting place in the branches of the tree of life, to defend us and strengthen us with the love flowing through the branches. And as we are nestled there, all that we bear is transfigured in the resurrection so that we become places of glory.

For more than a thousand years, massive stone crosses have marked the places of glory in the lands of Celtic Christianity. These so-called high crosses stand like trees, ten to twelve feet tall, on sites of sacred activity, outside the earliest churches and monasteries, and on burial mounds. They are not only carved with the winding, interweaving lines that we associate with Celtic calligraphy, but each cross also displays scenes from numerous scriptural stories—the stories of salvation inscribed upon the cross of Jesus. A tree of life, indeed, as the tendrils of carved lines encircle the stories of God's faithfulness—of Daniel in the lion's den, Elijah taken up into heaven, Jonah in the whale, and Miriam and Moses at the Red Sea; stories of healing and exorcism; stories of preaching the word of life. All these describe to the viewer what the cross of Jesus has wrought, how in Jesus' life all our stories have a nesting place. As you look upon one of these high crosses, it is easy to allow the tendrils of this tree of life to come and embrace the stories of sacred love that we know, the complicated and bewildering stories of our own world, of our selves.

The tree of the cross is thus a meeting place. It is the place where our lives meet the lives of our forebears and their witness to the love of God in the midst of death. It is the place where we meet one another, where we can see one another anew as those in whom God's glory is revealed. The cross is where our lives are joined to God's life. The branches of the tree of the cross are thus a bridge that spans all the alienation and separation we experience, a bridge that stretches from person to person, and a bridge that we may picture allowing a connection between us when all else seems lost.

From the cross comes forth the community of the Church, as we find ourselves in this age and across the ages connected thus in the resurrection life. To this reality the evangelist John points most certainly when he tells how from the cross Jesus gives his mother to the beloved disciple and the disciple to his mother, and the disciple "took her into his own home" (John 19:27). Here we have the nucleus of community, that network of mutual love which in John's Gospel stems from Jesus, and most particularly from Jesus as he is lifted upon the cross. For as John also tells us, it is on the cross that Jesus draws and gathers all people to himself (John 12:32). And so nestled in this tree of life, this tree of the cross, we find our common life and all our connections one to another.

"Faithful cross! above all other, one and only noble tree . . . bend thy boughs, O tree of glory," to gather us and all the world into your most tender care.

We come before your cross, O Christ, unable to comprehend the vastness of a love that embraces all the pain and horror of this world, unable to speak fully our gratitude for your creative power at work in the midst of destruction and despair. Yet you are the God who wakens our hearts to the suffering around us and within us, and who teaches us to remember your ways of faithfulness. Give us the strength never to forget the harm we inflict on one another, never to forget the needs of those who are in anguish and distress, and above all never to forget that you are always with us, the God of our salvation and our hope. Amen.

Self-Giving Love
Good Friday

Meanwhile, standing near the cross of Jesus
were his mother, and his mother's sister, Mary
the wife of Clopas, and Mary Magdalene. When
Jesus saw his mother and the disciple whom he
loved standing beside her, he said to his mother,
"Woman, here is your son." Then he said to the
disciple, "Here is your mother." And from that
hour the disciple took her into his own home.

John 19:25–27

There's a story about an old man who used to
spend hours and hours in his village church,
just sitting in front of the crucifix with his eyes wide
open, doing nothing. One day his priest visited him
at home and asked him, "What is it that you are
doing all these hours when you sit in church, in front

of the crucifix?" And the old man said to the priest, "I look at him. He looks at me. And we are happy."

Our ancestors in the faith, like most people in the ancient world, believed that you could take things into your body through your eyes, by looking at them, just as we also take food and nourishment in through our mouths. That is, when you gaze upon something particularly beautiful or noble or loving, it becomes a part of you. So they (as we do also) went to church and gazed upon the icons and pictures of the saints in order to let that holiness enter their bodies. They went on pilgrimage to the Holy Land to gaze upon the place of Jesus' birth, of his suffering and crucifixion. By looking attentively, prayerfully at those locations of the outpouring of divine love, they believed that the same love would enter their bodies—through their eyes—and shape their lives.

It is indeed this understanding that lies behind our practices of gazing at the events of Jesus' suffering and death in the Stations of the Cross, or when we gaze upon the presence of Christ in the Blessed Sacrament, praying that Jesus' tremendous love might enter our bodies and shape our hearts and actions. "I look at him. He looks at me. And we are happy."

The Gospel of John has a great concern with "seeing": seeing the signs that Jesus does, seeing the revelation of God, and in particular seeing Jesus, the Son of Man, lifted up on the cross. In John's theology the cross is the showing forth of God's glory—glory because everything that it means to be God, the fullness of grace and truth, compassion and justice, is present in the all that it means to be "flesh": vulnerable, mortal, subject to violence and shame, at risk of abandonment and despair. But here, the evangelist John says, God is most fully present, here divine love is utterly engaged with humanity. And it is as though the Gospel of John has been training its hearers for this moment, stressing the importance of seeing from the very beginning, "And the Word became flesh and lived among us, and we have *seen* his glory . . . full of grace and truth" (John 1:14, emphasis added). Jesus, in his words to his followers, has consistently directed their gaze (and thus ours) toward his being lifted up on the cross. It is not sight alone, but rather "recognition," seeing in the cross—the lifting up—its true meaning: healing poured out for a world torn by suffering, life for all, and the gathering of a humanity alienated from the ground of its being. The cross in John's Gospel is displayed as the focal point of all the longing and desire of humanity, drawing our gaze. "When I am lifted up from the earth, I shall draw all people to myself," Jesus says about his own death (John 12:32 AT).

Thus the evangelist John brings his hearers to this scene with the four women and the beloved disciple standing near the cross, gazing presumably upon the one whom they loved and who is now "lifted up." It is a remarkable scene, laden with significance for John, for us. John tells us that Jesus sees the mother and the beloved disciple, meets their gaze, and then he speaks, to the mother: "Woman, behold your son," and to the beloved disciple, "Behold your mother." (Our translations may say, "Here is your son, here is your mother," but in Greek it is clearer, "Behold, see, your son; see, your mother.") With this word from the cross, Jesus directs their gaze away from him, away from the cross, and toward each other. It is as though he says, "Now that you have recognized the presence of God, faithful, constant, in the midst of the worst that humans can do, now look upon each other and find that same wonder of divine love binding you to each other. See here the glory of God 'full of grace and truth.'"

But there is more here than simply the graceful truth that we see God and Christ in one another.

No, for John this is a moment rich in symbolism. The unnamed beloved disciple, the one who has reclined against Jesus' breast (John 13:23), just as Jesus is pictured as reclining against the Father's breast (John 1:18)—this beloved disciple is emblematic of the whole Johannine community. And this community is here born anew, born from above, from Jesus lifted up on the cross—born to the mother. It is a moment of birth—of the recognition of adoption. "Son, look at your mother. Woman, look at your Son." Here in this word from the cross the Johannine church is born. And this birth from above means that the DNA of the cross, as it were, the formative pattern of self-giving love is meant to fill every bond of connection between one person and the next. "A new commandment I give to you," Jesus said, "that you love one another as I have loved you" (John 13:34 AT).

Let me put it another way. Sometimes when people come to me to talk about their lives, their prayer, their longing for God, their struggles for deeper knowledge of God, they come to a point in the conversation when they bump up against something that seems terribly difficult for them to speak about, some memory, some realization, some question that seems too hard to utter. And so they dance

around it, or fall into an awkward half-silence.
Then, if I am attentive, if I am grounded in the
mercy of God, I sometimes find myself picturing the
cross thrown down as a bridge between us, span-
ning the distance, creating a nucleus of community,
and grounding our conversation in the self-giving
of love uttered from the cross. As I gaze upon that
cross, I find myself praying in that moment that the
cross will be a sure sign of the defense God offers us
in the face of all that we fear, that the cross will be
an assurance of the creativity of God, of God's presence in the midst of a truth that seems too hard to
bear, a suffering that feels too deep to name. And I
find myself silently uttering thanks to the God who
traverses all the distances between one person and
another, the God who in the cross spans the gaps
and reconciles us one with another; I utter thanks
to the God who gives us to each other.

For the word from the cross, "Woman, behold
your son; Son, behold your mother," is a word that
says we are brought together by God's initiative—
brought together in intimacy and brought together
as strangers and friends—by God's initiative. This is
God's creativity from the cross: to form a household,
to form a community of faith and love—chosen and
nurtured in the pattern of freely self-giving love,

born not of blood, nor of the will of the flesh, nor of human will—but born of the willing, the desiring, of God (John 1:13), born into a community of resurrection love, a love stronger than any death.

> *O Jesus, beloved friend and savior, as we gaze upon your cross this day, allow our gaze to meet yours; allow us to see you transfigured not only in your suffering but also in your compassion for the whole world. May we take that same love into ourselves and find our bonds with one another remade in the patterns of the mercy and justice you have established from the foundation of the world. May we be born anew into the community of your risen life. Amen.*

A Good Soaking

Easter Day

When the sabbath was over, Mary Magdalene,
and Mary the mother of James, and Salome
bought spices, so that they might go and anoint
him. And very early on the first day of the week,
when the sun had risen, they went to the tomb.
They had been saying to one another, "Who will
roll away the stone for us from the entrance to
the tomb?" When they looked up, they saw that
the stone, which was very large, had already been
rolled back. As they entered the tomb, they saw
a young man, dressed in a white robe, sitting on
the right side; and they were alarmed. But he said
to them, "Do not be alarmed; you are looking
for Jesus of Nazareth, who was crucified. He
has been raised; he is not here. Look, there is the
place they laid him. But go, tell his disciples and
Peter that he is going ahead of you to Galilee;

there you will see him, just as he told you." So
they went out and fled from the tomb, for terror
and amazement had seized them; and they said
nothing to anyone, for they were afraid.

Mark 16:1–8

L ook there, the Christ, our Brother, comes re-
splendent from the gallows tree, and what he
brings in his hurt hands is life on life for you and
me."[5]

In the last few days, I have been watching the rain
soak into the ground. My little garden thirstily drinks
up the rain water; the rich dark soil of the nearby
fields is sodden. The bright green new shoots of the
perennials and bulbs appear almost to dance with
joy at such an abundant soaking; the life that has
lain hidden in the ground all winter is revealing itself. And in this wet, rainy Easter I rejoice, although
truly it is not an Easter on which the earth matches
the radiance of God's glory with the bright splendor of sunshine. This is an Easter on which I pray
that the grace and power of Jesus' resurrection will
not simply warm us and brighten our lives as spring
sunshine does, but that this outpouring of love will
soak into our hearts and souls, just as the rain soaks

into the earth. As the prophet Isaiah prayed, so we do also, "Drop down, you heavens, from above, and let the skies pour down righteousness; let the earth open, and let it bring forth salvation."[6]

Water is one of the primary symbols of Easter— water and light. Since the eighteenth century, the Church has tended to talk about the resurrection primarily in terms of light, but from ancient times, Christians have told the story of Jesus' resurrection and of the life it gives by talking about water. We remember how God led the people of Israel out of slavery in Egypt *through* the waters of the Red Sea; we remember how the people crossed the waters of the Jordan River and entered the Promised Land. With the words of the psalms, we sing of how God delivered the beloved ones from the waters of death, the torrents of oblivion: "All your rapids and floods have gone over me," "but you have saved me, O Lord, from deep waters" (Ps. 42:9; 18:17 AT) A wet, soaking passage from death to life. And our ancestors in the faith spoke of how God tenderly cared for them in the difficult times and how God cared for Jesus even as he descended into the depths of death; they remembered how God gave their ancestors water in the wilderness, quenching their thirst by a miraculous spring of water from the rock (Num. 20:1–13; Ps. 78:15–16). And in all generations, we have spoken of our longing for God as thirst: "As the deer longs for the water-brooks, so longs my soul for you, O God. My soul is athirst for God, athirst for the living God" (Ps. 42:1–2). So the water that falls all around us reminds us of the water of life, the grace and love that God pours out upon creation.

The Gospel does not tell us what the weather was like that morning when the three women—Mary Magdalene, the other Mary, and Salome—went to the tomb to anoint the body of Jesus. Perhaps it was a drenching morning; perhaps the flow of their tears as they grieved for Jesus and lamented this violent, terrible death soaked the earth as well as their faces. But as they come to the tomb, they find it open and empty, except that when they look inside they see a young man dressed in white—a heavenly messenger of some sort—who tells them simply not to be troubled and that Jesus, the crucified one, whom they seek, is not there, but has risen and gone before them into Galilee as he told them he would.

Here in Mark's Gospel—at least in its earliest forms—this is all that we are told about Jesus' resurrection. Mark does not tell us about how Jesus appeared to the women or the other disciples; rather

Mark tells us only that Jesus, the crucified one, is risen and goes before us. It is enough, because Mark simply wants us to know that God brings Jesus through suffering and death, and that death is not the end of the story.

But Mark also wants us to trust that it is through Jesus' suffering and death that we see God most fully and it is through Jesus' death that we receive life. As the psalmist sings, "Though I walk through the valley of the shadow of death, I shall fear no evil; for you are with me" (Ps. 23:4). Mark invites us to honor, even treasure, the places of suffering and injustice, the difficult passages through which we have gone, the murky nights of the soul, our trembling and our tears—not simply to rejoice when we are on firm ground in bright sunlight. We honor them not because they are right and good, but because they are places where God has been with us, though we may not always have known it; we honor them because Jesus has knit them all into his suffering, redeemed them by his death. The crown of thorns has flowered upon Jesus' brow; his sorrows heal our own.

So Saint Mark turns our attention to the crucified one this Easter. Saint John the Evangelist, in his turn, takes up this way of understanding the resurrection, when he tells us that we recognize the risen Jesus by the wounds in his body, by the imprint of the nails (John 20:20). The resurrection does not erase Jesus' suffering or ours. Instead, all the suffering is wrapped in love, enfolded in God's compassion, soaked in the saving, healing waters of grace. The miracle of Easter is not that Jesus rose from the dead, but that Jesus' risen life continues to be with us, to be with our world, and to soak into our thirsty souls and bodies. Jesus comes to us from the cross, comes to us as one who knows the deep aches of our hearts, and holds out to us his hurt, wounded hands—and what he holds in his wounded hands is life for us. The crucified and risen Jesus offers us life, this enlivening love that carries us through all the difficult and painful passages.

We come this Easter to the waters of baptism; perhaps at church today you too will watch water pouring into the font. And if you do, your community, like mine, will bless it by retelling the story of how God saves us through water and by telling how Jesus leads us, by his dying and rising, into resurrection life. Each in our own places, we shall remember how our lives have been made one with Jesus in his death through the water, and that we also share in Jesus' risen life. From the earliest days of the Church,

Easter has been a time—the time—for baptism, for here Jesus touches us with his wounded hands and gives us true life. Easter is the night of new birth: a watery, grace-filled birth.

There are two crucial consequences of this gift of life: the first is that by your baptism you can know that God, the creator of the universe, loves you with a love that is stronger than death, and that nothing you ever do will separate you from God and nothing anyone will do to you can separate you from God. The loving God is always with you—no matter what. You are the beloved of God!

Second, because we know God through the crucified and risen Jesus, who understands everything it means to be a human being, you can bring everything you feel and think and experience to God, and God will hold it with love, tenderly, remaking all your broken places and giving you a new start. With this God there is always hope. If you ever lose your way, remember that you bear on your forehead the sign of the cross, which tells you that you belong to this loving God. You won't be perfect or have a life that is always happy and easy and sunny, but as you go from day to day, keep remembering this God who made you and who loves you fiercely. What Jesus brings is "life on life for you and me."

And so, we give thanks for the wondrous gift of love and life that the crucified Jesus gives us with his wounded hands. Let it soak into your hearts so that hope, compassion, and a deep trust in the goodness of God may spring up like the green plants in the springtime. Alleluia! Christ is risen!

> *The mystery of your death and resurrection, O Lord, sustains our lives and restores the world in which we live. Each day you hold out to us the gift of life, the possibility of mercy, and the means of living in you. Help us to live in the strength of this wondrous reality, so that our hearts may grow in hopefulness and thankfulness as we share in your new creation. Amen.*

II
Resurrection Words
The First Week of Easter

On the Threshold

Monday in Easter Week

After the sabbath, as the first day of the week was dawning, Mary Magdalene and the other Mary went to see the tomb. And suddenly there was a great earthquake; for an angel of the Lord, descending from heaven, came and rolled back the stone and sat on it. His appearance was like lightning, and his clothing white as snow. For fear of him the guards shook and became like dead men. But the angel said to the women, "Do not be afraid; I know that you are looking for Jesus who was crucified. He is not here; for he has been raised, as he said. Come, see the place where he lay. Then go quickly and tell his disciples, 'He has been raised from the dead, and indeed he is going ahead of you to Galilee; there you will see him.' This is my message for you." So they left the tomb quickly with fear and great joy, and ran

to tell his disciples. Suddenly Jesus met them and
said, "Greetings!" And they came to him, took
hold of his feet, and worshiped him. Then Jesus
said to them, "Do not be afraid; go and tell my
brothers to go to Galilee; there they will see me."

Matthew 28:1–10

In these six meditations for the first week of Eastertide, I invite you to explore with me how Jesus'
resurrection informs our engagement with God in
prayer. In each reflection, as I take up a different
Gospel story of how the risen Jesus came and met
his friends, his disciples, I suggest how the resurrection enables us to bring our lives more deeply,
more intimately to God. That is, how might these
stories provide means whereby we are more able
to "pray our lives"?[7] I ask this question out of the
sense that, for Christians, the resurrection provides
a groundwork for all our prayer: we pray in the
hope of renewal, restoration, and reconciliation that
God makes real in Jesus' resurrection. I begin this
exploration today with the moment of greeting, of
encounter and recognition.

In comparison to the rich and complex stories
in the Gospels of Luke and John of the risen Jesus'

appearances to the women and the other disciples, Matthew's story is remarkably sparse. Matthew expends his narrative art on the description of the "angel of the Lord," the stunning effect on the guards, and the angelic message to Mary Magdalene and the other Mary. But when Jesus appears to the women, the account is swift and restrained. He has but one word for them, "Greetings!" and to this their reply is that typically Matthean response to the recognition of the enigmatic presence of God: they come and they worship. Then Jesus sends them on their way with the same message the angel already gave them: "Go and tell my brothers to go to Galilee; there they will see me." I want to save for another day the second part of what Jesus says, "Go . . . tell," and today to attend to the first word, "Greetings!" It is the simple, everyday word that opens any conversation, the word that begins the encounter, recognizes the presence of the other, and brings the relationship into being here in this moment. "Greetings"—we greet with other words, perhaps, or with the intensity of a glance, a bow of the head, a clasp of the hands, a kiss—but it is the practice that opens up the hospitable space between one person and another. And here it is the risen Jesus who speaks it, who initiates, who creates the moment of gracious welcome in which the women recognize Jesus, in which their lives, their bodies and souls, are drawn into worship.

You might be accustomed to think of your prayer as beginning with yourself, with your own voice reaching out to God, awaking God as though from slumber, and calling God to your aid, to attend to your need. And such prayer is indeed an important and honored movement of the heart, voiced out of our deepest need and frustration at the sometimes seeming absence of God. But you might also consider your prayer as entering into that hospitable space opened up by the risen Jesus' greeting to us. It is as though the whole universe is resonating at every moment with divine greeting, and you have only to respond. And you may pause, just here on the threshold, as it were, to savor the greeting, to know yourself recognized and welcomed. Our prayer— our habits of bringing our lives to God—begins then with the divine initiative that shows us the space for our lives within the life of God.

In Matthew's story it is the crucified Jesus whom the women seek. And it is the crucified Jesus, now risen, who greets them. In his story of Jesus, Matthew shows us that the one in whom the mercy and justice of God are embodied is therefore the one whom death cannot hold. The compassionate and just purposes of God are constant and pervasive, stronger than the powers of destruction and violence. The word of greeting, spoken by the risen Jesus, is thus a word spoken out of an awareness of the depth of human suffering, a knowledge of the worst, and an assurance of the faithfulness of God. It is a greeting that creates a space into which we can bring our awareness of pain, betrayal, and corruption, as well as our hope and our delight. It is a greeting that welcomes our lives, that invites us to utter the reality of who we are, however confused and chaotic that may be, and thus to pray our lives. So hover here on the threshold for a while; savor the word of greeting that the risen Jesus speaks this day to you.

> *Lord Jesus Christ, live out in us—in all that we are and have yet to become—the full mystery of your death and resurrection. Help us to yield all by showing us and teaching us to welcome all, especially the dark guest within our soul. Stretch and transform us by the power of your love, that we may find ourselves in you and see ourselves in you, and in your beauty. Amen.[8]*

Easter Tears

Tuesday in Easter Week

But Mary stood weeping outside the tomb. As she
wept, she bent over to look into the tomb; and
she saw two angels in white, sitting where the
body of Jesus had been lying, one at the head and
the other at the feet. They said to her, "Woman,
why are you weeping?" She said to them, "They
have taken away my Lord, and I do not know
where they have laid him." When she had said
this, she turned around and saw Jesus standing
there, but she did not know that it was Jesus.
Jesus said to her, "Woman, why are you weeping? Whom are you looking for?" Supposing him
to be the gardener, she said to him, "Sir, if you
have carried him away, tell me where you have
laid him, and I will take him away." Jesus said
to her, "Mary!" She turned and said to him in
Hebrew, "Rabbouni!" (which means Teacher).

Jesus said to her, "Do not hold on to me, because
I have not yet ascended to the Father. But go to
my brothers and say to them, 'I am ascending to
my Father and your Father, to my God and your
God.'" Mary Magdalene went and announced to
the disciples, "I have seen the Lord"; and she told
them that he had said these things to her.

John 20:11–18

W"oman, why are you weeping?" Is it a reproach? Is it a word of comfort? Or, rather,
is it a question that searches out Mary's plight and
the reason for her tears? "Why are you weeping?"
With this question, first the angels and then the risen
Jesus reach across the threshold and draw Mary into
conversation. I want today to explore this resurrection question as an invitation for our prayer, as a
question that can be integral to our life with God.

In the Middle Ages, preachers were expected to
make their congregations laugh regularly during the
fifty days of the Easter season. This "Easter laugh-
ter" was one of the practices by which the faithful
expressed their sheer joy in the resurrection: joy and
delight, the ringing out of Alleluias, a certain light-
ness of heart with which all respond to the promised

gift of life and the renewal of hope. What room
is there here for weeping, for mourning and lamentation? "Woman, why are you weeping?" It is a
question that has often been taken as a criticism, as
though Mary's tears (and ours) are a sign of faith-
lessness, of not remembering Jesus' promises, of
looking in the wrong place or in the wrong way.
Such a reproof is more like Luke's story: "Why are
you seeking the living among the dead? Do you not
remember?" But here in John's Gospel, there is no
reproach, just the question, "Why are you weeping?" that invites Mary to speak. And we should
be clear too that Mary is not weeping simply because she has found the tomb empty and the body
of Jesus gone; no, she has been weeping since she
first came and stood outside the tomb, before she
ever looked in. John's ancient audience would recognize Mary's actions immediately: she has come to
the place of burial to lament. The tomb is the ritual
location of women's lamentation, lamentation not
so much as the sheer outpouring of emotion, but
lamentation as the community's traditions of plac-
ing their beloved dead amid the memory of the
promises of God. We may imagine Mary not simply
weeping, but crying out to God with the words of
the psalms, the laments, such as Psalm 88:11–12,

"Do you work wonders for the dead? Will those who have died stand up and give you thanks? Will your loving-kindness be declared in the grave? your faithfulness in the land of destruction?" Such prayer springs forth from a life shaped by long experience of bringing one's fears and sorrows to God. Such lamentation springs forth from the ground of knowing a God whose love is stronger than death.

"Why are you weeping?" This is a question addressed as well to us, to invite our prayer. You may have your own reasons for weeping in these days— a new awareness of mortality, a relationship gone awry, hopes disappointed, the sharp grief of recent loss, or the dull ache of old sorrow. Or it may be that in the strength of what you know of divine love you have breathed in the sorrows and pain of the world, entering in solidarity into the suffering of another, a friend or a stranger. We could lament for many hours, enumerating the effects of violence and hatred in our world. The question, "Why are you weeping?" invites us not only to speak of our own sadness, but also to name before God the pain of others, to let our hearts be moved with compassion and with deep passion for justice.

It is a resurrection question because it is in the deep knowledge of God's faithful commitment to life that we can look into the darkest and seemingly most hopeless places of our lives and our world. It is a resurrection question because our prayer utters our need for God in the face of God's creativity. And it is a resurrection question because our capacity to be moved with compassion, to enter into the need of another, to ask another "Why are you weeping?" is itself rooted in God's movement toward us, to share our lives and to restore our hope. Let this resurrection question search out your soul, your loves, your commitments, that you may speak your life to God.

> *Hear our prayer, O God, and let our tears*
> *come before you, an offering of compassion*
> *for a suffering world, a remembrance of our*
> *hope in you, and a sign of our longing for jus-*
> *tice. Restore us, O God of hosts; restore your*
> *people, that our tears may strengthen us to*
> *be signs of your mercy and faithfulness all*
> *our days. Amen.*

Mystery Meeting Mystery
Wednesday in Easter Week

Now on that same day two of them were going to
a village called Emmaus, about seven miles from
Jerusalem, and talking with each other about
all these things that had happened. While they
were talking and discussing, Jesus himself came
near and went with them, but their eyes were
kept from recognizing him. And he said to them,
"What are you discussing with each other while
you walk along?" They stood still, looking sad.
Then one of them, whose name was Cleopas,
answered him, "Are you the only stranger in
Jerusalem who does not know the things that
have taken place there in these days?" He asked
them, "What things?" They replied, "The things
about Jesus of Nazareth, who was a prophet
mighty in deed and word before God and all the
people, and how our chief priests and leaders

handed him over to be condemned to death and crucified him. But we had hoped that he was the one to redeem Israel. Yes, and besides all this, it is now the third day since these things took place. Moreover, some women of our group astounded us. They were at the tomb early this morning, and when they did not find his body there, they came back and told us that they had indeed seen a vision of angels who said that he was alive. Some of those who were with us went to the tomb and found it just as the women had said; but they did not see him." Then he said to them, "Oh, how foolish you are, and how slow of heart to believe all that the prophets have declared! Was it not necessary that the Messiah should suffer these things and then enter into his glory?" Then beginning with Moses and all the prophets, he interpreted to them the things about himself in all the scriptures.

As they came near the village to which they were going, he walked ahead as if he were going on. But they urged him strongly, saying, "Stay with us, because it is almost evening and the day is now nearly over." So he went in to stay with them. When he was at the table with them, he took bread, blessed and broke it, and gave it to them. Then their eyes were opened, and they recognized him; and he vanished from their sight. They said to each other, "Were not our hearts burning within us while he was talking to us on the road, while he was opening the scriptures to us?" That same hour they got up and returned to Jerusalem; and they found the eleven and their companions gathered together. They were saying, "The Lord has risen indeed, and he has appeared to Simon!" Then they told what had happened on the road, and how he had been made known to them in the breaking of the bread.

Luke 24:13–35

A long and elegantly crafted story Luke tells us today—but Eastertide is a time for storytelling, not only with the ancient stories about the risen Jesus, but also in speaking of our own lives and our deepest hopes. We speak of how the faithful creativity of God engages our memories and our yearning, how our hearts burn within us. Luke's story this morning is about the interpretation of Scripture, how a stranger—we know him to be the risen Jesus—comes alongside the two on the road and interprets the events of their lives, their great sorrow, through his way of drawing out the law and the prophets. Luke's fine story most likely encapsulates the scriptural practices of his community: their habits of reading the Scriptures of Israel as speaking of Jesus, their traditions of telling the story of Jesus' death and resurrection through the medium of the psalms, the Torah, and the prophets. And although Luke ties everything up very neatly—a little too neatly—and although his community's reading practices might not be ours (I do not think, for example, that on its own terms Hebrew Scripture speaks of Jesus), I want to explore what it means to read Scripture, to pray with Scripture as part of our living into the resurrection.

The stranger asks the two on the road, "What are you discussing with each other as you walk along?" Or more literally, "What words are you tossing back and forth as you walk?" This is another resurrection question that, like the one we looked at in yesterday's reflection, "Why are you weeping?" searches out the hearts and minds of the two disciples. It asks them to speak of their quandaries, their questions, their sorrow, their disappointments—and they do. They tell the stranger what is in their hearts.

When we read Scripture, when we study it critically, when we pray with Scripture, it is—I would suggest—a process of *mystery* meeting *mystery*. The more time we spend with Scripture, the further we go, the more complicated it becomes. We discover the world of the text, the worlds of the texts, to be multifaceted, multidimensional, even foreign at many times. What appears at first to offer simple answers instead opens up myriad questions. We experience the ambiguity of what we read; we experience ambivalence about the perspectives we discover. But what a rich treasury! What a fascinating, mysterious city to explore!

But you and I are also mystery—each of us similarly a rich treasury, multifaceted and multidimensional. You do not come to the text as an empty vessel waiting to be filled, but with a heart and mind full of memories and experiences, commitments and doubts. You come with the knowledge of what delights you, and with your experiences of wounding, betrayal, injustice, failure. You come to the text as someone who lives *now*, here in this place. The mystery that you are, indeed the mystery that abides in the heart of each of us, meets the mystery of the text—and the two converse. And as your reading of Scripture, your praying with Scripture takes place in the company of others, together we can be drawn into how the mystery of another meets the mystery of the text. In my experience, moreover, it is a conversation less about answers and more about discovery, about voicing our questions, describing what we seem to discover, offering it to another, and having our hearts stretched by what our neighbors discover.

This is a conversation that every step along the way opens out onto an encounter with God—a God who is not contained in any text, yet glimpsed in all—a God to whom our questions can always point, a God who is indeed the grounds of our questioning, a God who asks us, "What are the words that you are tossing back and forth as you walk along?"

> *Blessed Lord, who caused all holy Scriptures*
> *to be written for our learning: Grant us so to*
> *hear them, read, mark, learn, and inwardly*
> *digest that we may embrace and ever hold fast*
> *the blessed hope of everlasting life, which you*
> *have given us in our Savior Jesus Christ, who*
> *lives and reigns with you and the Holy Spirit,*
> *one God, for ever and ever. Amen.*[9]

Have You Anything Here to Eat?

Thursday in Easter Week

While [the disciples] were talking about this, Jesus himself stood among them and said to them, "Peace be with you." They were startled and terrified, and thought that they were seeing a ghost. He said to them, "Why are you frightened, and why do doubts arise in your hearts? Look at my hands and my feet; see that it is I myself. Touch me and see; for a ghost does not have flesh and bones as you see that I have." And when he had said this, he showed them his hands and his feet. While in their joy they were disbelieving and still wondering, he said to them, "Have you anything here to eat?" They gave him a piece of broiled fish, and he took it and ate in their presence.

Then he said to them, "These are my words
that I spoke to you while I was still with you—
that everything written about me in the law
of Moses, the prophets, and the psalms must
be fulfilled." Then he opened their minds to
understand the scriptures, and he said to them,
"Thus it is written, that the Messiah is to suffer
and to rise from the dead on the third day, and
that repentance and forgiveness of sins is to be
proclaimed in his name to all nations, beginning from Jerusalem. You are witnesses of these
things. And see, I am sending upon you what my
Father promised; so stay here in the city until you
have been clothed with power from on high."

Luke 24:36–49

Have you anything here to eat?" This is the question the risen Jesus poses this morning. "Have
you anything here to eat?" I love this homely, down-
to-earth question—a question a close friend might
ask, not presuming on hospitality; a question a child
might ask a parent. It is a question that Luke uses here
to place emphasis on fleshly, bodily resurrection: this
Jesus is no apparition, this Jesus has flesh and bones,
this Jesus can eat broiled fish. Luke is here sorting

out options about resurrection, making sure his audience understands that the new life Jesus brings has to do with real human bodies that need food, real bodies that need hope. Luke's conviction here reaches deep into the songs of Israel—as the psalmist proclaims life beyond the grave, "My heart, therefore, is glad, and my spirit rejoices; my *body* also shall rest in hope. For you will not abandon me to the grave, nor let your holy one see the Pit" (Ps. 16:9–10, emphasis added). God's purposes for us include our bodies, ultimately refashioned into resurrection bodies—as Paul emphasizes—but bodies that are even now objects of divine concern, divine compassion.

"Have you anything here to eat?" One Maundy Thursday I was coming back from downtown Boston on the subway. The man beside me as we were getting on the train at Charles Street Station was carrying in his hand a plastic bag of sliced bread. Just as we boarded the train, a fairly unkempt homeless man approached him, pointed at the bag of bread and then at his own mouth. The man beside me pulled away sharply at first; then in an instant he turned and looked at the man and handed him the whole bag of bread.

"Have you anything here to eat?" This is a resurrection question for our prayer and our work, recalling us to the task of bringing before God in prayer the very real bodily needs of others (as well as of ourselves): the need for food, for shelter, for clean water, for safety from violence. And our prayer needs also to be a place where we grow into deeper awareness of such very real bodily needs—to hear in our prayer the voices that say, "Do you have anything here to eat?" and to see the hands that point to the bag of bread we are carrying.

Because our prayer is dynamic, engaged with the purposes of God, it seldom stops at the naming of need. Rather it expands into our action, overcoming our fear and resistance, quickening us to respond with our own bodies—our own hands and feet, our flesh and bones—to the very real bodily needs of others. Our prayer quickens us to give of our own material resources, to devote our work not to what perishes but to what gives real nourishment—to body and soul and mind—even to search out how our work participates in the remaking of the world and of society, even in the little corner that we are given to tend.

"Have you anything here to eat?" This is a resurrection question that invites us to extend to those around us the same divine hospitality that has welcomed us, for we might find in the face of another—

the flesh and bones of another—the presence of a divine stranger, the presence of the Lord of Life—and it might just be useful to have some broiled fish on hand.

> *Blessed are you, O Lord God, creator of the universe, for you give us food to sustain our bodies and hope to quicken our hearts. Give us the gift of attentiveness to the bodies and spirits of all your creatures, and grant that we may find you in one another and serve you by serving one another. Amen.*

A Riot of Fish

Friday in Easter Week

After these things Jesus showed himself again to the disciples by the Sea of Tiberias; and he showed himself in this way. Gathered there together were Simon Peter, Thomas called the Twin, Nathanael of Cana in Galilee, the sons of Zebedee, and two others of his disciples. Simon Peter said to them, "I am going fishing." They said to him, "We will go with you." They went out and got into the boat, but that night they caught nothing.

Just after daybreak, Jesus stood on the beach; but the disciples did not know that it was Jesus. Jesus said to them, "Children, you have no fish, have you?" They answered him, "No." He said to them, "Cast the net to the right side of the boat, and you will find some." So they cast it, and now they were not able to haul it in because there were so many fish. That disciple whom

Jesus loved said to Peter, "It is the Lord!" When Simon Peter heard that it was the Lord, he put on some clothes, for he was naked, and jumped into the sea. But the other disciples came in the boat, dragging the net full of fish, for they were not far from the land, only about a hundred yards off.

When they had gone ashore, they saw a charcoal fire there, with fish on it, and bread. Jesus said to them, "Bring some of the fish that you have just caught." So Simon Peter went aboard and hauled the net ashore, full of large fish, a hundred fifty-three of them; and though there were so many, the net was not torn. Jesus said to them, "Come and have breakfast." Now none of the disciples dared to ask him, "Who are you?" because they knew it was the Lord. Jesus came and took the bread and gave it to them, and did the same with the fish. This was now the third time that Jesus appeared to the disciples after he was raised from the dead.

John 21:1–14

I f you visit the northern Italian town of Aquileia, close to the coast of the Adriatic and once, in Roman imperial times, an important harbor, you will find a beautiful basilica, built in the fourth century CE. A mosaic floor stretches from one end of the basilica to the other—a mosaic filled with depictions of fish, dolphins, crustaceans, and almost every sort of sea creature imaginable. Here and there angels are fishing from small boats; partway up the nave you find Jonah and the whale: the story that, for many early Christians, became a way to speak of Jesus' death and resurrection. Fish, fish everywhere, fish even in trees—a riot of fish. And one can imagine a congregation of fishermen, sailors, boat makers, and net makers singing the praises of God, offering their prayers on this wondrous carpet of multicolored fish. And with a further stretch of the imagination, one might envision them standing and hearing this resurrection story about the miracle of a net full of fish. The decorative pattern of this church, as so often in late antique churches, speaks of the abundance, the eucharistic abundance, available to those who share in the divine life. Being in this church offers a foretaste of heaven, a vision of the hospitality and generosity of God.

"Children, you have no fish, have you?" This question, posed in John's Gospel to the disciples by a stranger on the beach, reaches into the experience of limitation, failure, and seemingly fruitless labor. It is a question that John uses to highlight the paradoxical instruction from the risen Jesus that the fishermen put in their nets in more or less the same spot where they had been fishing, without result, all night. It may be that at this point John is in dialogue with Luke's Gospel—stressing that the broiled, barbequed fish breakfast that the risen Jesus shares with the disciples, the food for the meal in which they recognize him, is itself given as the gift of God. Luke had, after all, used a similar story early in his Gospel to make the point that true discipleship was that which responded to the paradoxical, often nonsensical call of God, and that the result of such discipleship was abundance beyond human imagining (Luke 5:1–11). But John wants to go further and say that this abundance of life is the gift of the resurrection, not simply the consequence of obedient discipleship. "I came that they may have life, and have it abundantly," promised the Johannine Jesus to his followers (John 10:10). Throughout the Fourth Gospel, John stresses the initiative of God precisely in the place of human limitation and seeming failure: the cross. For John the cross is the revelation of God's glory, the place for the gathering of humanity into the generosity of God.

"Children, you have no fish, have you?" Like the other questions of the risen Jesus, this question searches out our need. It asks us to speak in our prayer of our frustration and our sense of limitation—there is only so much one fragile body can do, only so much one group of people can take on. It asks us to speak, perhaps only with a tired, mute sigh, of our exhaustion, of the times when we are at the end of our rope in trying to stay constant and loving in a relationship that tries our patience (a child? an aged parent? a trying employer?). This resurrection question asks us to tell God about all those situations when we have spent ourselves seemingly to no avail. It invites us to admit, to God at least, those occasions when we feel hopeless and despairing at the plight of the world: the unending violence, the economic injustice, and our own apparent inability to effect real change. It asks us even to speak of the times when our prayer itself seems fruitless, pointless.

The risen Jesus may not come visibly to us to speak a word of instruction. But that is why we have stories, why we have the memory of grace. Like the mosaic floor of the basilica in Aquileia providing a glimpse of the abundance of divine life, this story of the wondrous haul of fish and of divine generosity is available to spark our imaginations so that we might envision, even in the times of greatest frustration, God's movement toward us and God's initiative in our lives. It is a story into which we may dip our nets again and again and find them filled with hope, the hope that God promises to give us life and to give it abundantly.

> *Blessed are you, Lord God, creator of the universe; blessed are you for the fish of the sea. Blessed are you for the work that you give us; blessed are you for the wondrous gift of heavenly life. Blessed are you for the hope that you give us each moment; blessed are you for ever and ever. Amen.*

Loosening the Roots

Saturday in Easter Week

Now after [Jesus] rose early on the first day of the week, he appeared first to Mary Magdalene, from whom he had cast out seven demons. She went out and told those who had been with him, while they were mourning and weeping. But when they heard that he was alive and had been seen by her, they would not believe it.

After this he appeared in another form to two of them, as they were walking into the country. And they went back and told the rest, but they did not believe them.

Later he appeared to the eleven themselves as they were sitting at the table; and he upbraided them for their lack of faith and stubbornness, because they had not believed those who saw him after he had risen. And he said to them, "Go into all the world and proclaim the good news to the whole creation. The one who believes and is baptized will be saved; but the one who does not believe will be condemned. And these signs will accompany those who believe: by using my name they will cast out demons; they will speak in new tongues; they will pick up snakes in their hands, and if they drink any deadly thing, it will not hurt them; they will lay their hands on the sick, and they will recover."

So then the Lord Jesus, after he had spoken to them, was taken up into heaven and sat down at the right hand of God. And they went out and proclaimed the good news everywhere, while the Lord worked with them and confirmed the message by the signs that accompanied it.

Mark 16:9–20

On Good Friday, after the liturgy and other services of the day were over, I was speaking with an old friend, and I asked him how he had spent the first part of the day. He told me how he had taken the day off from his work and had spent it readying his garden for spring. And then he said, "My hands are very tired." And as I looked curiously at him, he explained how most of his gardening that day had been devoted to digging up a large patch of day lilies and Siberian iris and pulling apart the roots and bulbs of the one from the other, separating and dividing the lilies and the iris, loosening their roots—part of the necessary work of spring. And I thought of how much of my modest attempts at gardening is spent loosening the roots of plants to remove the weeds binding them, that they might grow freely and abundantly.

An ancient sermon from the early church speaks of the reasons why we contemplate the Passion of Jesus: it is "to loosen the roots of compassion within our hearts." I have found myself much drawn to this image over the last weeks. Compassion, of course, not only for the suffering of Jesus, but more important, for those around us, the stranger and the friend. For compassion is at the base of all that we can offer another: that movement of the heart into solidarity with the suffering, the struggle of another. And there in that solidarity we may find the insight and the impulse toward what it would be to move toward and work toward freedom: freedom from suffering, freedom from death and decay, freedom from injustice, freedom from deceit—freedom indeed from all that binds and imprisons us—the freedom that is both the promise and the real gift of the resurrection. Where is it that you sense the need for freedom for your heart or your actions? Where do you find your compassion hemmed in and root-bound? Our hearts are willing—they want, I dare-say, to grow abundantly in this compassion—but at times we may find that the roots of our compas-sion are tangled, impacted, and constrained, bound by hesitation, convention, the palette of our fears, a lack of vision, our own grief, or our exhaustion and sense of limitation. All that we encounter as we pray with the resurrection—as we allow the words of the risen Jesus to speak in our hearts as we have throughout this week—enables the roots of com-passion to be loosened within ourselves—to do this springtime gardening work.

The words of the risen Jesus in Mark's conclud-ing summary of resurrection appearances, "Go into all the world and proclaim the good news to the whole creation," does not so much search our hearts as send us out over the threshold of encounter. It is the counterpart to the greeting that first welcomes us into encounter and into divine hospitality. This "lon-ger ending" of Mark's Gospel, added most likely in the second century, lists remarkable signs—strange perhaps to our ears—that will be done by the believ-ers, those who partake of resurrection life: exorcism, snake handling, drinking poison unharmed, speaking in tongues, healing. To the ancient religious mindset, those would all have been recognized as acts of *freedom,* acts of loosening people, loosening creation from all that binds and constrains—freedom from the power of death, the powers and principalities, freedom from demons, curses, spells—freedom even from *fate* itself. This freedom, this unbinding, resounds from one New Testament text to another as the gift of the resurrection. And because we have glimpsed, tasted, such loosening in the encounter with the risen Jesus, because the roots of our compassion have been loosened—even just a bit—this word is for us: "Go . . . proclaim . . . work toward . . . enact this good news—of lasting freedom—to all creation."

O Lord of compassion, Lord of freedom, you greet us and welcome us. Your questions search our hearts and minds, your generosity draws us into the abundance of life, your presence nurtures us, and now you send us forth to live this life, to proclaim freedom from every evil, every bond of fear and injustice: keep us ever mindful of your love and strengthen us to live your risen life. Amen.

III
Incorporating the Resurrection

Longing and Abiding
Tuesday in Easter Week

But Mary stood weeping outside the tomb. As she wept, she bent over to look into the tomb; and she saw two angels in white, sitting where the body of Jesus had been lying, one at the head and the other at the feet. They said to her, "Woman, why are you weeping?" She said to them, "They have taken away my Lord, and I do not know where they have laid him." When she had said this, she turned around and saw Jesus standing there, but she did not know that it was Jesus. Jesus said to her, "Woman, why are you weeping? Whom are you looking for?" Supposing him to be the gardener, she said to him, "Sir, if you have carried him away, tell me where you have laid him, and I will take him away." Jesus said to her, "Mary!" She turned and said to him in Hebrew, "Rabbouni!" (which means Teacher).

Jesus said to her, "Do not hold on to me, because
I have not yet ascended to the Father. But go to
my brothers and say to them, 'I am ascending to
my Father and your Father, to my God and your
God.'" Mary Magdalene went and announced to
the disciples, "I have seen the Lord"; and she told
them that he had said these things to her.

John 20:11–18

If you have traveled up the coast of New England,
passing through one seaport after another, you
will probably have noticed any number of large late-
eighteenth- and early-nineteenth-century houses
overlooking the harbors and bays. Many of these
houses have, at their very tops, small, square porches
fenced around by a railing. Known as the "widow's
walk," this architectural feature is said to be distinc-
tive to the houses of sea captains (and their wives).
The widow's walk evokes the lonely, longing gaze
of the sea captain's wife, scanning the horizon each
day that she might see the sails of her husband's
long-overdue ship returning from its ocean voyage.
It evokes the uncertainty, the risk, and the joy of
reunion that were knit into the life of these coastal
towns, sending forth onto the high seas their sons

and fathers, their uncles and nephews, sometimes their daughters (as a young woman, my grandmother went to sea from Nova Scotia with her aunt and sea captain uncle to care for their children aboard ship). And the figure of the woman, lonely on the house-top, wondering if her beloved has been lost in the depths of the sea, if he has wandered away forever into a far-off land, becomes in coastal tradition a focal point for the rhythms of loss and mourning, for the storms of life, as well as for the constant possibility of return and reunion. As a Scottish folksong from a similar way of life goes: "How often haunting the highest hilltop, I scan the ocean thy sails to see. Wilt come tonight, love, wilt come tomorrow, wilt ever come love to comfort me?"[10]

The ancient audience for whom the evangelist John crafted this story of Mary Magdalene in the garden would have recognized in Mary similar patterns of longing, uncertain grief, and persistent hope. John takes this story, already held and long honored within his community's tradition, and shapes it to speak of the means by which his listeners might be drawn deeper into mutual love and how they might continue to "abide"—that particularly Johannine way of life—in the face of Jesus' death. The ancient audience, steeped in traditional

practices of death and mourning, would have recognized that Mary came to the tomb that morning
to do two things. They would have seen first that
Mary came to lament, that is, to enter into those
communal practices of grieving for the dead, so that
the grief welling up within her would take its place
amid the griefs and hopes of her ancestors, so that
her longing and sadness would be articulated in the
traditional language of lament, perhaps the words
of the psalmist, "Why are you so full of heaviness,
O my soul? and why are you so disquieted within
me? My tears have been my food day and night,
while all day long they say to me, 'Where now is
your God?'" (Ps. 42:6, 3). They, like most ancient
(and modern) inhabitants of the Mediterranean,
would have recognized that Mary was doing the
work proper to the women of her community, the
work of lamenting the dead and of finding within
that lamentation the seeds of hope, for the psalmist
goes on to say, "Put your trust in God; for I will yet
give thanks to him, who is the help of my counte-
nance, and my God" (Ps. 42:7).

This ancient audience would have gone on to recognize that Mary came also to the tomb to remember.
John names the grave not simply as a burial place,

but with the ritually poignant term *mnêmeion,* "the place of memory" or "the place of remembering." The place of burial for the beloved, honored dead was in the ancient world one of the principal places of remembering, the place to which you returned again and again to speak of one buried there, perhaps to eat a meal or to pour a liquid offering onto the grave, but above all to remember. And thus it was that the grave became a place where stories grew, not only from speaking of the person's life but also out of the practices of lamentation, so that the words of the ancient promises and prophecies came to wrap around this very particular memory of the sharp, recent loss. And indeed our stories about Jesus may well have grown in part out of these practices of remembering at the place where he was buried.

But Mary remains at the tomb that morning, even after she finds that the tomb has been opened and the body of Jesus is gone, even after the other disciples have disappeared. John's ancient audience would then have recognized one thing more: that in remaining, Mary was risking an encounter with one whom we might call one of the "restless dead."[11] John tells this story with all sorts of hints—the garden with its tomb is just the sort of place where heroes come back to life and appear to their devoted followers, to converse intimately with them; this garden is just the sort of place where heroes come back to life to exact just vengeance on their oppressors and those who dishonor them. It is a risk to remain in such a garden. You might be called by your name; you might be recognized; you might be drawn into fresh and enigmatic relationship with one whom you thought you knew; you might be given such clarity as to see the world anew.

Lamentation, remembrance, and the risk of encounter: I want to suggest these three as facets of resurrection life, of abiding in love. To lament is most likely not what we associate first with Eastertide, with resurrection joy. But while we may not be weeping for Jesus, there is something about resurrection that allows us to recognize with greater clarity the needs of the world, to face into the darkest and most dire aspects of society. Resurrection faith proclaims that God's loving purposes to restore, reconcile, and re-create are constant and unshaken: this is our hope! Love is stronger than death! And such strength enables us to see more clearly, to speak more forthrightly of what needs to be redeemed and refashioned.

This strength enables us to lament. Resurrection love moves our hearts to lament the destruction of peoples, the decay of a society, the power of an oppressor, the habits of deceit and betrayal—to lament not as those without hope, but to lament in order to uncover the promises of hope in the very midst of the worst that humans can do to one another. And this resurrection love strengthens our hearts not only to speak of our own sorrows, our deep griefs and tragedies, but also to move with compassion into solidarity with the griefs of others. Resurrection love allows us to breathe in with compassion the sufferings of one another.

And remembrance: as we stand with Mary Magdalene in the place of lamentation, the place of remembering, we too remember. As we lament for a broken and suffering world, we remember before God all those who need God—in John's Gospel it is the Paraclete, the Spirit, who brings all things to remembrance, not just the things about Jesus, for the Paraclete causes us to remember one another in compassion. This Johannine Spirit working within us brings ourselves to our remembrance, our pasts, sometimes what we would rather forget, but above all, the ways in which God has sought us out and shown us deepest compassion, abundant nurture. And so our lives become places of remembering, perhaps particularly in the places where we thought there was only death and decay, for out of our awareness of such love, we too begin to form a story, to let the promises and prophecies of hope wind around the story that we tell of our lives—a resurrection story.

And we too may join Mary at the place of remembering to risk an encounter, an encounter with the Lord of Life, for as we bring our lives into remembrance, as we expand our lament and our compassion, we deepen our engagement with one who appears in surprising and enigmatic ways (a gardener? a stranger on the road? over broiled fish at breakfast?!). In prayer, across the dinner table, in the words of one whom you find frightening or difficult to love, as you read, tonight, tomorrow?— you do not know when the risen Jesus will speak your name, drawing you to share afresh in the resurrection purposes of God, inviting *you* to share in divine creativity for the redemption of the world. This is the risk we take: the risk of encountering God, the risk of God remembering us, the risk of the risen Jesus recognizing us in the garden of our lamentation, the risk of encountering the truth about ourselves and about our world, and above all the wondrous truth of the trustworthy and steadfast love of God.

Give us courage to encounter you, O risen Lord: courage to stand in solidarity with those who suffer, courage to hope in your faithfulness, and courage to give of ourselves for the well-being of others. And as we do so, may we find our true selves, knit into your death and resurrection, named as your beloved, and grateful for all that you are working within us. Amen.

Ask and Receive
The Second Sunday of Easter

When it was evening on that day, the first day
of the week, and the doors of the house where
the disciples had met were locked for fear of the
Jews, Jesus came and stood among them and
said, "Peace be with you." After he said this, he
showed them his hands and his side. Then the
disciples rejoiced when they saw the Lord. Jesus
said to them again, "Peace be with you. As the
Father has sent me, so I send you." When he had
said this, he breathed on them and said to them,
"Receive the Holy Spirit. If you forgive the sins of
any, they are forgiven them; if you retain the sins
of any, they are retained."

But Thomas (who was called the Twin), one
of the twelve, was not with them when Jesus came.
So the other disciples told him, "We have seen
the Lord." But he said to them, "Unless I see the

mark of the nails in his hands, and put my finger in the mark of the nails and my hand in his side, I will not believe."

A week later his disciples were again in the house, and Thomas was with them. Although the doors were shut, Jesus came and stood among them and said, "Peace be with you." Then he said to Thomas, "Put your finger here and see my hands. Reach out your hand and put it in my side. Do not doubt but believe." Thomas answered him, "My Lord and my God!" Jesus said to him, "Have you believed because you have seen me? Blessed are those who have not seen and yet have come to believe."

Now Jesus did many other signs in the presence of his disciples, which are not written in this book. But these are written so that you may come to believe that Jesus is the Messiah, the Son of God, and that through believing you may have life in his name.

John 20:19–31

As carefully as a gardener lays out a garden, as skillfully as a sculptor brings out the shape and beauty of the stone, so the Gospel writer John arranges his story of Jesus' life. Each word, each event is chosen and carefully placed so that it resonates with meaning and picks up the themes of other stories.

We encounter in this Gospel story the disciples gathered together in a room on the evening of the resurrection. They have heard what Mary Magdalene had to say to them, that she had seen the Lord, but they do not yet speak and go about freely. They are afraid, and their hearts are troubled. And we find them in this room, with the doors shut. I think that John must want us and all his readers to cast our minds back to that other evening just four days before (the one we celebrate as Maundy Thursday), when the disciples were also gathered in a room—gathered on the evening before Jesus was arrested. These two evenings, these two gatherings of disciples, are carefully placed, one on each side of the crucifixion. The cross stands at the center of John's Gospel, for in John's understanding of Jesus, the cross is where we see Jesus most clearly and in the greatest glory. And in these two evening gatherings of the disciples, we discover how the gift of the cross, the gift of life, is given to us.

On the evening before he was crucified, Jesus gathered his disciples, and at dinner washed their feet, providing in this action an example of love that touches and cares for us where we are most vulnerable. He gives the disciples a commandment, that they should love one another as he has loved them (John 13:1–35). Jesus is here equipping his followers with the essentials, with what they will need to continue to do God's work in the world, to be bearers of God's life and love for the world. And in John's Gospel, Jesus speaks to his disciples that evening at great length, telling them many things about their relation to him and his relation to God, assuring them that they are gathered into this community of mutual love. Jesus gives them "peace," for he says, "Peace I leave with you, my peace I give to you" (John 14:27). As though looking ahead to the evening of the resurrection, John has Jesus say, "You will have pain, but your pain will turn into joy. . . . You have pain now; but I will see you again, and your hearts will rejoice, and no one will take your joy from you" (John 16:20–22).

We hear now the story of that second evening, the evening of the resurrection, when the risen Jesus comes and stands among the disciples; he stands in the midst of their pain, their grief, their fear. And he speaks one thing to them: "Peace be with you." The gift of peace, which he gave them before his resurrection, is the bond that joins them together; it is the connection by which they recognize that he is Jesus. And so too with us, as we say to one another "Peace be with you," we claim the fundamental connection that exists among us and with Jesus; we express how we have been joined together by Jesus. As the disciples, as we, recognize Jesus with us, pain and sorrow turn to joy.

On that evening before he was crucified, Jesus also promised his followers the gift of the Holy Spirit to remain with them, to comfort and encourage them, to teach them, and to lead them into truth. And here on this evening of the resurrection, the promise is fulfilled: Jesus breathes on them and says, "Receive the Holy Spirit." The gift of the spirit is not only a comfort but also a commission—Jesus sends forth the disciples to continue to offer life to the world. In John's Gospel Easter and Pentecost are one and the same day!

It would seem then that all is well, that the world is full of peace and joy, recognition and reunion. But there is a problem: not all the disciples were there that evening; the circle of love is not complete. Thomas is missing. Do you remember those folktales, like Sleeping Beauty, in which someone is left off the invitation list for the party to celebrate the princess's birth, but turns up to curse the child? Well, although he doesn't curse anyone, Thomas seems to me a bit like such a character, turning up later angry and stubborn, refusing to believe unless he too sees Jesus risen from the dead, unless he puts his hands into Jesus' wounds.

I must admit that I am a great fan of Thomas's. I treasure the way in which he does not hesitate to say what he needs in order to believe. Too often this "doubting Thomas," as he is frequently called, has been used to discourage questions, to squelch the explorations that lead to deeper faith. And this does Thomas a disservice, just as much as it wrongly discourages our questioning. It is important as we hear the story of Thomas to remember that ours is a faith that seeks understanding and has plenty of room for questions and doubts.

The key to understanding Thomas is to return once more to that evening when Jesus gathered his disciples before his crucifixion. After he has promised that their pain will turn to joy, he says, "On that day you will ask me no question. Very truly, I tell you, if you ask anything of the Father in my name, he will give it to you. . . . Ask and you will receive, so that your joy may be complete" (John 16:23–24). Now the disciples, on the evening when the risen Jesus comes into their midst, do not indeed ask him any questions. But it is Thomas who asks and Thomas who receives. Thomas asks for what he needs: to see the mark of the nails, to put his hand in Jesus' wounds. It is this that Jesus gives to him, inviting him to touch his wounded hands and side. "Ask and you will receive, so that your joy may be complete." And Thomas believes, recognizing the crucified Jesus, now risen, as his Lord and his God.

We too receive with Thomas and through this story one of the greatest gifts of the resurrection: that it is the crucified Jesus who is risen. Thomas, and we in turn, recognize Jesus by his wounds, not only by his splendor. The joy of the resurrection includes the full memory of the pain, the loss, the grief, the harm inflicted. And this is essential if we are to recognize the presence of Jesus with us today, because we can look not only to the places of hope and rejoicing to find Jesus but also to the wounded places of the world and our lives. For it is especially there—in suffering and hurt, in weakness and need—that Jesus is present.

That it is the crucified Jesus who is the risen Lord is also vital if the resurrection is to be something more than a comfort in our own lives, if it is to empower us. For Jesus did not die a simple death at the end of a long, full life (though such deaths are full enough of sorrow and loss), but Jesus' wounds remind us that Jesus died as an executed criminal, unjustly put to death in his innocence. They remind us that his death comprehends hatred, violence, horror, shame, and political maneuvering; his death contains sin and evil at its worst. That such death could not destroy God and God's purposes is radically good news, because it means that nothing is outside the power of the resurrection. It means that the resurrection not only gives you and me eternal life, but that the resurrection is somehow at work everywhere. The wounded hands of Jesus carry the frightful genocides around the world, the bodies of those maimed and killed by war, and the souls ripped apart by hatred and prejudice; they cradle the homeless and hungry—his hands have felt the nails of injustice, the chains of oppression; the wound in his side bears the mark of senseless violence and the careless harm humans inflict on one another. But the wounded hands of Jesus are also, as the hymn says, building in us a new creation.[12] When we see that it is the crucified, wounded Jesus who is risen, when we place our hands in the wounds of the world where Jesus is found today, we find hope; then we can believe anew. For if God is there, God who is the fountain of life, true hope exists for the rebuilding and restoration of creation.

So ask—ask each day, each moment—for this life. "Ask and you will receive, so that your joy may be complete."

> *Spirit of the risen Christ, come pray in us the prayer we need this day. Teach us to pray, relying on your promises and your trustworthiness. Teach us to find abiding joy in your presence among us, a joy that comprehends all pain and loss. Teach us the ways of peace, a peace that remakes our fractured relations, a peace that comes from entrusting our lives to you. Breathe your prayer within us that we may abide in you all the days of our lives. Amen.*

The Pathways of Grace

But you are not in the flesh; you are in the Spirit, since the Spirit of God dwells in you. Anyone who does not have the Spirit of Christ does not belong to him. But if Christ is in you, though the body is dead because of sin, the Spirit is life because of righteousness. If the Spirit of him who raised Jesus from the dead dwells in you, he who raised Christ from the dead will give life to your mortal bodies also through his Spirit that dwells in you.

So then, brothers and sisters, we are debtors, not to the flesh, to live according to the flesh—for if you live according to the flesh, you will die; but if by the Spirit you put to death the deeds of the body, you will live. For all who are led by the Spirit of God are children of God. For you did not receive a spirit of slavery to fall back into fear, but you have received a spirit of adoption. When we cry, "Abba! Father!" it is that very Spirit bearing

witness with our spirit that we are children of
God, and if children, then heirs, heirs of God and
joint heirs with Christ—if, in fact, we suffer with
him so that we may also be glorified with him.

Romans 8:9–17

Have you ever said, "I know the way so well
that I could go there in my sleep"? Since I was
a child, I have spent some part of every summer,
sometimes the whole summer, sometimes only a
week or so, at the same house far down east on
the coast of Maine. The house sits high on a granite bluff overlooking the ocean, and for the past
thirty-five years, I have been carefully picking my
way on the sloping ledges, through the juniper and
bay bushes, down to the edge of the shore. My right
foot in this crevice here, a hand on this pine tree for
balance, a big step over the slightly slippery boggy
spot there—and knowing all along where it might
be worth looking for ripe blueberries. Each year,
as I return to the place, I am surprised at how the
memory of the pathway lives in my body, and how
without much conscious thought I make my way
from the house to the water's edge by the same familiar route. I find that the path is inscribed within

me, and each twist bears as well the memories of what I have found and done at that spot.

Perhaps you too have an experience like this, in a regular walk you take, in your path for doing errands, in the way you move about the place where you live—a way known so well that you could follow it in your sleep. Not only is the route familiar, but sometimes too our paths through our world recall for us stories, stories of our past, of who we are, and of the encounters and conversations and events that have shaped us. It may not be entirely positive, of course: we may find that our body, our flesh, surprises us by the way in which it bears the memory of a rape, an attack, or repeated abuse, even though on another level of knowing, we have come to terms with that experience. The story of the way over which we have come is held and told in part by our flesh—written in our mortal bodies.

Or it may be less in how our bodies move through the world and more in a particular sensory experience: the remembered feel of another's body, a taste that recalls us to a time at our grandparents' dinner table, or a smell. The ancients spoke much more of the *smell* of holiness than we do, referring to the sweet smell of a garden, the rich odor of myrrh and frankincense, the scent of balsam-bearing oils, all as emanating from the body of a saint, from the place of prayer and contemplation, as well as from the richness of the eucharistic liturgy. And perhaps you know a little of this, recognizing that "church" smell—the mixture of oils and polish, good candle wax and flowers, perhaps a whiff of incense, and a bit of mustiness and damp from stone and wood that emanates from a well-loved and well-used church building. And it can be a smell that causes us to remember our own experience of prayer and godly community and draws us into prayer—the remembrance, even for a moment, of God's activity and grace. Whatever it is, as we discover the familiar pathways, the bodily memories that bring us home to God, as it were, we may treasure them, go over them again and again so that they become inscribed more deeply. It is what musicians and others call "kinesthetic memory": the practiced movement of the hands at the keyboard, so that the memory of how the music goes is written into the pathways of the body and becomes, as it were, "natural."

Paul, in writing to the various Christian groups in Rome, engages in an intricate description of life in Christ, of how we in our baptismal life reveal the justice and the glory of God. By the midpoint of the letter, he is concerned with what it is to live a life bound up with Jesus' death and resurrection, what it means to live "in Christ." Throughout this epistle, Paul develops a contrast between two stories, two ways of life, two dominions or kingdoms. One is the story of how sin and death, which sin has co-opted, dominate the world and how together they have come to colonize human existence, holding everything and everyone in their thrall. Paul uses the language of political and military action to characterize how sin takes over, holding creation, like a subject people, in its web of obligation and indebtedness.

The other story that Paul develops in Romans is the story of Jesus' death and resurrection. To put Paul's theology in a nutshell, it is this event that breaks the dominion of sin, releases humanity and all creation, and thus allows us to live under a reign of grace and freedom. Paul's point is that by baptism we move from one story to the other, from one way of understanding the world to the other. In baptism the story of Jesus intertwines with our own story, making what is true of Jesus true also of us, namely, that we will be given life, that the Spirit of God lives in us, and that out of our present sufferings, true glory will shine forth. And we are given this life in and through our mortal bodies, not apart from them.

For Paul, baptism is the doorway through which we move into a new world. We leave a world in which the predominant story told is one of the power of sin and of alienation from God and one another, a story of slipping ever deeper into despair, a story in which death has the last word. And we enter a world where the defining story tells of the re-creation of our bodies, of hope for the remaking of the structures of society, of being at peace. We leave a story that tells of rebellion against God, a pattern of making gods out of things that cannot give life and hope, and we are gathered anew into a story of our intimacy with God, of our becoming beloved members of God's household. We leave behind a way of looking at the world that sees it as a place of constantly impending punishment, a place where we must live in fear. And in its place, we are given a view of the world that knows it as a place pulsating with God's compassion and mercy, a world crowned with God's goodness—for us as well as for all others. Being gathered into the life of Christ crucified and risen allows our lives to be shaped and formed by the story of God's mercy.

Now much of the purpose of Paul's Letter to the Romans—indeed of a great deal of Christian preaching—is to remind those who have been gath-

ered into this story of what is true about them. It
is a matter of calling to remembrance the passage
from one way of understanding the world to another, and of retelling, helping us all to remember
the story of creative, saving love. Paul does this
in what we have heard today almost by means of
shorthand, a shorthand that may present certain
obstacles to us. He contrasts life "in the flesh" with
life "in the Spirit," saying to his listeners, "But you
are not in the flesh; you are in the Spirit, since the
Spirit of God dwells in you." *"Flesh"* here stands for
that entire story of rebellion against God, of the
domination of sin, fear, and punishment; it stands
too for our susceptibility to the domination of sin,
perhaps because it is often our flesh that reminds
us of the limitations of our created existence and
hence becomes a primary location of our struggle
against our mortality and our createdness. "Flesh"
does not stand in any simplistic way for our bodies,
and we who are trying desperately to recover our
entire created beings as a place of holiness must be
clear about this and about the fact that to use "flesh"
in this way is probably not so helpful for us. For
Paul the body is integral to all of human life: it is
integral to our mortal life, for the way in which
we form godly community, and to our transformed

existence after death, for how we participate in the life of glory. Our mortal *bodies* will be given life; indeed—as Paul goes on to say—we await the redemption *of* our bodies, not redemption *from* our bodies.

Forgiving Paul for the way in which he uses "flesh"—if indeed it remains problematic for us—and bearing in mind that Paul is always trying to help us remember the story of our salvation, we may ask how our bodies can remember the story of God's compassion and mercy. How can we bear in our bodies the memory that we are gathered into the resurrection of the crucified Christ? How does our flesh know that it is the dwelling place of the Spirit? How is the memory of salvation inscribed upon our bodies, so that we know with every cell of our created being that we live in the power of the resurrection?

"When we cry 'Abba! Father!' [or if we prefer, 'Amma, Mother'] it is that very Spirit bearing witness with our spirit that we are children of God, and if children, then heirs, heirs of God" (Rom. 8:15–17). Paul turns here to our longing, as that which is most basic to our prayer, our orientation to the source of freedom and life. The other day I watched a pool of barnacles as the incoming tide flowed over them: their tentacles reached wildly upward, through their open shells, to catch every particle of plankton and whatever else barnacles eat. So too is our longing, if we attend to it, to catch every whisper of divine love, every particle of grace amid the tide of God's presence flowing over and around us. This is at the foundation of our prayer, as we reach with our whole lives—with all the concerns and joys, the commitments and sorrows that we bear—to absorb something of resurrection life. And this we do with the whole of our selves, not through some pure spirit isolated from the entirety of the way we move through the world. Our longing, as well as our loving, happens with and in our mortal bodies: we pray with our aches and pains; we know our limitations muddled up with our deepest desires; our mindfulness of God happens as we stand, footsore, at the bus stop or enjoy the comfort of our favorite chair.

Perhaps a story will help. One summer a colleague and I took a group of students to study early Christian monuments in Italy. As it happened, the trip coincided with the hottest June Italy had experienced in a hundred and fifty years, and this meant that as we visited the famous basilicas and baptisteries and inquired into their origins, theologies, and social contexts, we did so bathed in sweat,

sometimes faint from the heat, and constantly thirsty
no matter how much water we drank. Our longing for understanding, our explorations, our contemplation, and from time to time our prayer, all
took place in our bodies, with more awareness than
usual of their limitations and mortal natures. And
it was in our mortal bodies that we received life—
those glimmers of beauty, insights into our ancestors' witness to the compassion and mercy of God,
flashes of knowledge and understanding—all fore-
tastes, I would say, of resurrection life, all answers
in some way to our longing.

To practice the embodiment of our prayer, the
mortal grounding of our longing for God, helps us
live in the strength of the resurrection. In addition, it
helps us respond readily to the real needs of others,
because compassion often entails the willingness to
get our hands dirty, to smell unpleasant smells, to
suffer in bearing the pains of another. This mutual-
ity of "bear[ing] one another's burdens" (Gal. 6:2)
lies at the heart of how Paul understands the resurrection life, flowing forth from the common meal
of the community, the proclamation of the Lord's
death (1 Cor. 11:23–26). And so the practice of being in godly community (with our mortal bodies
and the mortal bodies of those we care about and

those we find difficult) is intertwined with the acts of compassion toward one another and with God's compassion toward each of us.

It is through such prayer, such mindfulness of God, and such compassion that resurrection life becomes written upon our bodies, so that the pathways of grace are ones that we know in our sleep, as in our waking, and so that we remember always that we are God's beloved ones.

> *Most gracious God, you have brought us from bondage into freedom, from despair into hope, and from death into life. You have marked our souls and bodies with the pathways of grace so that we may always find our way to you. Make us attentive to your ways with us, the ways of death and resurrection, so that by contemplating this mystery, we may find the roots of compassion ever loosened within our hearts and so share in your love for all the world. Amen.*

Notes

1. Hymn 370, verse 4, in *The Hymnal 1982* (New York: Church Publishing, 1985).

2. Hymn 166, verse 4, of *Pange lingua,* in *The Hymnal 1982.*

3. *Itinerarium Egeriae* 37.2.

4. This prayer is a central theme in *The Showings* (or *The Revelations of Divine Love*) of Julian of Norwich, but see especially chapter 3 of the "Short Text."

5. Hymn 197, verse 1, in *The Hymnal 1982*; words by John Bennett.

6. Advent antiphon on the Magnificat, based on Isaiah 45:8; see Howard Galley, ed., *The Prayer Book Office* (New York: Church Hymnal Corporation, 1994), 80.

7. The phrase is drawn from chapter 22, "Prayer and Life," of *The Rule of the Society of Saint John the Evangelist, North American Congregation* (Boston: Cowley, 1997), 45.

8. Based on a prayer of the Most Reverend Frank T. Griswold III, in "The Time To Pray Is Now: A Personal

Prayer Folder for the Episcopal Church and Its General Convention, Denver 2000," (Orlando, FL: Anglican Fellowship of Prayer, 2000).

9. Collect for Proper 28, in the Book of Common Prayer 1979 (New York: Church Publishing, 1979).

10. "The Boatman, or Fhir a bhata," traditional Gaelic song, translated by Thomas Pattison, in *The Songs of the North, Gathered Together from the Highlands and Lowlands of Scotland,* 2d ed.; ed. A. C. MacLeod and Harold Boulton; arr. Malcolm Lawson (London: Cramer, between 1869–1899), 48–50.

11. The phrase "restless dead" is taken from the title of Sarah Iles Johnston's study *Restless Dead: Encounters between the Living and the Dead in Ancient Greece* (Berkeley, CA: University of California Press, 1999).

12. Hymn 598, verse 4, in *The Hymnal 1982;* words by Walter Russell Bowie.